Love Letters to Life

OSHO

Love Letters to Life

150 Life-Transforming Letters by Osho

"Be a little more poetic. Write beautiful love letters to life.
That's what meditation is all about."

OSHO

These letters were originally published in Hindi as *Antarveena*. The
complete OSHO text archive can be found via the online OSHO
Library at www.osho.com/library

OSHO MEDIA INTERNATIONAL
New York – Zurich – Mumbai
an imprint of
OSHO INTERNATIONAL
www.osho.com/oshointernational

Distributed by Publishers Group Worldwide
www.pgw.com

Library of Congress Catalog-In-Publication Data is available

Printed in India by Manipal Technologies Limited, Karnataka

ISBN 978-1-938755-86-6
This title is also available in eBook format ISBN: 978-0-88050-074-6

Contents

Preface   vii

Letters 1-150   1 to 96

About Osho   97

OSHO International Meditation Resort   100

For More Information   103

Preface

You write that my words ring in your ears;
what I want is for their echo to carry you
into that space where everything is silent, empty.
This is the way from words to emptiness.
There one meets oneself.

I am in bliss.
Take my love
I have nothing else to offer, it is my only wealth.
The marvel of it is that the more of it you give
the more it becomes.
Real wealth is like that –
it grows as you give it away;
and if it diminishes, it is not wealth at all.

Osho
A Cup of Tea

1.

Love.

I received your letter when I returned from Delhi the day before yesterday. I am happy to know that you are experiencing bliss and contentment.

Bliss lives within us, but we do not find it because we are looking for it on the outside. Once the inner journey begins, new sources of bliss are continuously opening up.

In the kingdom of the inner, there is neither sorrow, nor pain, nor death. Once you reach this state of deathless you will be reborn, and you will cut all that binds you. Reaching this liberated state is the very goal of life. In this state, the self and the other drop, and only isness remains: without boundaries, indescribable; formless and figureless.

Before, there was the isness of "I"; now, there is the isness of the whole. Once this is attained, everything is attained. Once this is known, everything is known. Once you are in this state, violence and hatred, sorrow and pain, death and darkness – all will disappear, and what will remain will be *sat chit anand*: truth, consciousness, bliss.

May you attain *sat chit anand*. That is my wish.

2.

Love.

Truth is manifesting in every moment, in everything that is happening. It is being perpetually expressed. All that is needed are the eyes to see it; its light is ever-present.

I planted a sapling a year ago, now it has begun to flower. Before this happened there was a year of waiting.

Spiritual life is the same.

Be prayerful and wait – sow the seeds and wait for the flowers to come. Patience is the life-breath of meditation. Nothing can happen before its time. Everything takes time to grow.

I have received your letter. As you move on your journey you are forging a path between hope and despair. I am very happy to know this. The path of life is very winding – and it is good it is so. It creates a challenge for your courage and energy, and adds joy to the victory.

Only those who never set out on the journey can be called defeated. The one who sets out has already won half the battle. And the defeats that come in between are not defeats; they are only the backdrops against which the victories can stand out in their greater glory.

Existence is with you each and every moment; that is why attainment of the goal is certain.

I am in bliss.

3.

Love.

I am in bliss. I received your letter some time ago. Since then I have been away, hence my delay in replying. I have now returned after speaking in Indore and Shajapur.

One truth I witness every day is that one cannot live without spirituality. Without spirituality something in a person remains empty and unfulfilled. This emptiness will start to ache, but you will find no way to fill it. This is the state of modern man. I am not worried about it because in this state may lie the only hope for mankind's future and safety. Out of this very pain a thirst will be born, which, if given the right direction, can become a worldwide spiritual regeneration. For just as a dark night is followed by the rising sun, so the soul of man is very close to a new dawn.

News of this impending dawn has to be brought to every single person because it has to happen within each and every one of us. And we all have to make an effort for this dawn to occur. It will only come if we all make an effort. It cannot come by itself.

The birth of consciousness demands effort and patience. It is like birth pangs. This effort and waiting, these birth pangs, are not painful because through them the infinitesimal can open to the infinite. There is no greater bliss than giving birth to the vastness within oneself.

I am happy to know that you are moving toward the goal of life. If we just keep moving we are bound to reach.

May the divine be with you, that is my wish.

4.

Love.

I have received your letter and I am very pleased. It fills me with joy that you are touching new depths of peace and bliss! On life's journey there is nothing worth attaining other than this. When all else is lost, this wealth will still be with you. That is why it is, in fact, the only wealth; and those who have everything but this wealth are paupers – even with all their riches.

That is why one can be poor while having great riches, and rich while living in poverty, because such riches only give the illusion of destroying one's poverty. They don't destroy it, they only hide it, and this self-deception is very costly in the end, because a life that could have been an opportunity to gain some real treasure is spent uselessly living under this illusion.

It is very important to remain alert to the kind of wealth that is found on the periphery of life. For only those who realize its illusory nature will set out to search for the treasure that is hidden at the very center of life. Finding this wealth will destroy poverty forever, because such wealth can never be taken away from you, and only that which cannot be taken away from you is your own wealth, your personal wealth.

That which cannot be taken away cannot be found either, because that which can be found can also be lost. Inner wealth simply is. It is everywhere; one simply has to recognize it. In fact, to recognize it is to attain it. May every step you take in life lead you toward this wealth of wisdom – that is my wish.

I am in bliss. Give my love to all the beloved ones there.

5.

Love.

I am pleased with your very loving letter. May your flame of life rise smokelessly toward the truth – that is my only wish.

One has to turn one's life into a blazing fire in order to reach godliness. May you always remember this.

Asleep or awake, if this longing, this thirst, this remembrance, is in your every breath – if it is the whole focus of your vision – then nothing else needs to be done. Thirst, and thirst alone, is enough to attain it.

The ocean is so close, but there is no thirst in us. Its gate is so close, but we don't even knock. All that is needed is the ability to see that godliness is always present. But our eyes focus on other things, and our minds are filled with everything that is useless; that is why we are unable to see that which is.

The heart is covered with the other; that is why the self is forgotten. This covering has to be removed: the pondweed and the garbage strewn over the pure, clear waters of the lake have to be removed. Then we will see that we have never lost anything, that it cannot be lost. I am constantly living in truth, in isness. I am it. And so are you: *Tattvamasi*, Shvetketu. That art thou, Shvetketu. Wake up and remember. In all your actions, remember that which is watching them. In all your thoughts, let your focus be on that which is behind them. You have to awaken to that place where there is neither action, nor thought, nor movement. It is found beyond space and time. It is found where peace, bliss, and nirvana dwell. Once that is found, there is nothing further to attain. Give my love to all my beloved ones.

6.

Love.

I have received your letter that is filled with great love and your thirst for the truth. I am pleased.

Where there is so much thirst, attainment is not far away. If there is thirst, the path is being created. Truth is close by, like a light at the door.

The problem is not the truth, but of not having a seeing eye. It is not that your eye is missing. It is there, but it is closed.

It can be opened. Resolve and an effort toward constant spiritual discipline can open it. This eye is closed because of thoughts, the mind, and the smoke of passions. It will open when there is thought-less consciousness. Then the whole of life will be filled with light.

This is what I am teaching. I am teaching this pure state of thoughtlessness. I have no other teaching. If the third eye is open, it will teach you everything else.

To experiment with opening this eye, two hundred friends are gathering in Mahabaleshwar, Pune, on February 13th, 14th and 15th. It will be good if you can come. You will need to reach Mahabaleshwar by the evening of the February 12th.

My respectful remembrances to everyone.

7.

Love.

I am very happy to have received your letter. I was also immensely happy to meet you the other day.

The longing and thirst that you have for truth is a rare blessing. If it is there, then one day your jump into the ocean of meditation is bound to happen. I see you standing on the very shore – a simple jump is all that is needed.

The more meditation becomes natural, the more it is devoid of the tension of effort, the faster you will grow into it. It has to be practiced, but this should not become a tension and a preoccupation. I have called this approach "practice through nonpractice."

The impatience and restlessness that you may develop toward attaining the truth are the tension – the tension of effort. If there is infinite patience, tranquility and waiting, this tension of effort will disappear. Then, in the same way that flowers bloom naturally on the trees, constant growth will keep happening effortlessly and unexpectedly in *sadhana*, meditation.

Give my love to everyone there.

8.

Love.

Your first letter reached me in good time, but I was on a tour of Saurashtra so I could not reply. I received your second letter on my return. If you wish, I will be able to come. We will be able discuss your letters too, when you come here for the October camp.

If anybody can be helped in any way, I am ready to go anywhere. This is my only joy now.

The state of mind that you have described to me makes me very happy. You are moving in the right direction. Don't be worried about body postures and gestures. They will only help you, and then they will gradually disappear. Just practice a thought-less consciousness; all else will follow it like a shadow. If the mind is tranquil then whatever is happening is good.

The despair that you are feeling about life in general and what is happening is also transitory. This too will pass away. Then your service will be of real service.

We will be able to discuss all these matters in detail when we meet. Just remember that whatsoever is happening is the right thing, and its outcome too will only be helpful and good.

Accept my love. May existence give you light. That is my wish.

9.

Love.

I have received your letter. If consciousness,

self-realization, and awareness keep growing, then you are getting out of the hypnotic circle of the mind. If, on the other hand, unconsciousness and unawareness are growing, then you can be certain that the mind's sleepiness is deepening even more.

But without experimenting for yourself, nothing can be experienced. Do not go on thinking. Drop thoughts and enter within your self. Thought is nothing but the shore; the stream of life's energy is found in non-thinking meditation.

Kabir has said:

> *The seekers who have found it have dived deeply;*
> *Naïvely I began my search still sitting on the shore.*

10.

Love.

It is too long since I received your letter. All this time I have been constantly on tour; that is why I couldn't write even a few words in reply. My prayers, however, are always with you.

I am happy to know of the thirst and pain in your heart because they are the seed from which spiritual seeking is born.

Keep experimenting in your life in a quiet and natural way. Keep remembering that there is no soil which doesn't have a source of water lying beneath it, and there is no self which doesn't have a universal self within it.

Give my respectful remembrances to everyone there.

11.

Love.

In reply to your letter, I have been away. I came back

only the day before yesterday. I am now freed from the university, so traveling is my only life.

What is truth? Truth is a total experience of isness, of being, of one's life. The more the experience of isness is unconscious, the more untrue life is. Experience "I am" with the deepest intensity every moment. Let every breath be filled with it. Ultimately, the "I" will also disappear and only the "am" will remain. It is in this moment that "that which is" is known and lived.

Is dialogue possible in silence? In fact, dialogue is only possible in silence. Words say little and obstruct more. Deep down everything is connected. At this level of connectedness, feelings are transmitted in silence. Words are a very poor substitute for silent expression. The truth just cannot be said in words. It can only be expressed through the silent inner voice.

I am very happy with the advice that you have started giving me. Keep giving me such advice. After all, I know nothing about the world! I feel very touched by your care and love for me hidden within these words.

12.

Love.

I have received your letter. I am happy with your spiritual efforts and your reflections about them.

It is natural to worry about the present situation in this country, but the more you worry, the more it will become impossible to reflect. Worry and reflection are opposite poles. If you keep the mind silent, then gradually insights will begin to arise about what is worth doing. A peaceful mind spontaneously busies itself in the right way. Then the inner being becomes both the path and the light on the path.

I will not give you any advice on what you should do. My advice is to become absolutely peaceful. Once that has happened, your own being will start telling you what to do. It will always be right; there will be no possible alternative and you will have no doubts or apprehension. My advice is to live through insight, not thoughts.

If it is not possible, for health reasons, to sit for a long time while meditating then do it lying down. The question is not whether to sit or lie down. The real question is the state of your mind. Your journey is basically concerned with the mind, not the body.

For now, there is no meditation camp coming up. Let us see when I can be of help to you by being close.

Always feel my love with you. Give my respectful remembrances to everyone there.

13.

Love.

I was pleased to receive your letter.

What an intense longing for truth, peace and liberation you have! Feeling this longing, it seems that whatsoever I can do for you will be very small. Still, I want to help you to the fullest of my capacity.

Why do I want to do that? Perhaps not to do so is not under my control at all. I have to do that which existence commands me, and when I see you ready, I feel happy.

The moment when I will be able to show you the direction of your destiny is coming closer all the time. Yes, certainly write whatsoever you want to about yourself.

14.

Love.

I have received your letter and your questions.

I have purposely remained quiet about death because I want to awaken an inquiry about life in you. Those who ponder death reach nowhere – because how can death be known without dying? That is why the only outcome of such thinking will be either a belief that the soul is immortal, or that the end of one's life is a total end and nothing is left after it.

Both are simply beliefs. One belief is based on the fear of death, and the other on the idea that the end of the body is a total end. I don't want people to get entangled with beliefs and opinions, because that is not the dimension of experiencing, of knowing.

What, other than beliefs and dogmas, can be found by thinking about death? Thought never takes one beyond the known. Death is the unknown, so it cannot be known through thinking. I want to turn your attention toward life. Life is – here and now. One can enter it. Death is never here and now; either it is in the future or in the past. Death is never in the present. Has this fact ever come to your attention: that death is never in the present? Life is always in the present – neither in the past nor in the future. If there is life, it is now; otherwise it never is. So it can be known because it can be lived. There is no need to think about it. In fact, those who think about it will miss it because thought only moves in the past or the future; thought is not found in the present. Thought is a companion of death. In other words, thought is dead; there is no element of life in it.

Aliveness is always in the present – it *is* the present. Its manifestation is now, absolutely now; here, absolutely here. That is why there can be no thinking about life; there can only be experiencing – not an experience, but experiencing.

Experience means it has already happened; *experiencing* means it is happening. Experience has already become a thought, because it has already happened. Experiencing is thought-less, wordless, silent, void. That is why I call thought-less awareness the door to experiencing life. And the one who comes to know life comes to know all. He comes to know death too, because death is nothing but a misunderstanding born out of not knowing life.

One who does not know life naturally believes his body to be his very self. Because the body dies, the body perishes, the entity called the body disappears, the idea that death is a final end came into being. Those who are foolhardy live by this belief. The fear of death also comes from the fallacy of believing oneself to be the body.

Those who are suffering from this fear start chanting "The soul is immortal, the soul is immortal." In this way, the fearful and weak seek refuge. But both these concepts are born out of one and the same misunderstanding. They are two forms of the same misunderstanding and two different reactions from two different types of people. But remember: both types have the same misunderstanding, and in both cases the same misunderstanding is strengthened.

I don't want to give this misunderstanding any kind of support. If I say the soul is not immortal, then that will be an untruth. If I say the soul is immortal, then you will simply turn my words into a belief system and use it to escape from your fear of death – but those who live in fear will never be able to know the truth. That is why I say death is unknowable.

Know life. Only that can be known. And knowing life, immortality will also be known. Life is eternal. It has no beginning and no end. It manifests, it unmanifests. It moves from one form to another form.

In our ignorance, these points of transition look like death. But for one who knows, death is nothing more than changing your house. There is rebirth, certainly, but for me it is not a doctrine, it is an experience.

And I don't want to make it into a doctrine for others either. Doctrines have undermined the truth badly.

I want each and every person to know it for himself. No one can do this for someone else. But, because of doctrines, everyone seems to believe this, and everyone's individual search has become dull and dead. If you believe in doctrines and scriptures you can settle down quietly, as if you have neither to know anything for yourself, nor do anything about seeking the truth. This is utterly suicidal. That is why I don't want to have any part in this vast conspiracy which is killing man off by repeating doctrines. I want to turn all established doctrines upside down because, to me, this seems to be the only compassionate thing to do. In this way, everything that is untrue will be destroyed.

But truth is never destroyed; it is always available in its eternal freshness to those who are seeking.

Give my respectful remembrances to everyone there.

15.

Love.

You have been awaiting responses to your two letters; I

ask your forgiveness for the delay as I was extremely busy.

1. Expressions such as *avatar*, *tirthankara*, and *prophet* only indicate man's helplessness. This much is certain: some beings reach such a point in the upward journey of consciousness that to call them merely a human being is not meaningful. Yet one has to call them something or the other, so these expressions are used to describe man's transcendental states.

2. "Religious education" means to provide an opportunity for whatever is dormant within to awaken. Certainly, guides will be needed but they will be friends. The very effort of becoming a guru means someone will be imposed upon. Man must be saved from gurudom.

3. People in the past were similar. They were less educated so they could be exploited in every way. Their exploiters used to call the ease with which they could be exploited their simplicity. This was less simplicity and more stupidity. I am not a supporter of stupidity in any form. Simplicity that is the result of ignorance is not worth a paisa.
Only a simplicity born out of knowing has any spiritual value.
In the transition period, knowing brings cunningness. This is natural, but if mankind becomes well-educated, this transitory problem will disappear. And then the state of knowing, along with the simplicity that will follow it, will be all that is needed.

4. The poor are poor because their thinking is wrong.

Poverty is the result of our wrong thinking about life. That is why when there is a change in the way we see life, the social system will also change. Thinking systematizes. It is not for no reason that America is affluent. It is not for no reason that India is poor. Our philosophy is a philosophy of poverty. Their philosophy is a philosophy of affluence.

That is why I say that as long as our philosophy does not change, poverty will also not change.

5. Suffering happens neither to the body nor to the soul. Suffering happens to the combination of the two, that is, to man. Man is a combination of the two. The impact is on the body; the impact is physical. But the experience happens to the soul. The experience is spiritual. There can be no experience without an impact. There can be no perception of the impact without the experiencer. It is similar to the blind man and the lame man escaping and saving each other's lives from a forest fire. Separately, neither could have survived. Together, they both survived. Their union saved them, their coming together saved them. Such is the case with the experience of suffering.

6. An interest in metaphysics, in knowing truth, is in everyone. It doesn't matter who becomes the means toward its awakening. The means is secondary, only this much has to be kept in mind: the disciple is primary, the master is secondary. But gurudom teaches the opposite of this. My objection is simply that.

7. I have met Pandit Sukhlal. He is familiar with my books and talks. He has listened to many recordings of

my talks. I have seen one volume of his Hindi book, *Darshan Aur Chintan*.

8. Among Western thinkers, some similarity to my thought processes can be found in the existentialists; also in Zen seekers, the Sufi mystics, Krishnamurti and Gurdjieff.

My respectful remembrances to everyone there.

16.

Love.

I am pleased to have received your letter.

I know why you remained silent when you came to see me that day. Silence says much. What words fail to say, silence may manage.

You have asked about love and marriage. Love is perfect in itself. It desires nothing more. Marriage is the desire for something more. But where will you find this perfect love? Nothing on this earth is perfect. That is why love wants to become marriage. This is not unnatural, but it is certainly going to be troublesome, because love is the freedom of the sky and marriage is a bondage of the earth.

If one can be fulfilled by love, great! But who has ever been fulfilled by marriage?

Never escape from life. Escaping is suicide. Live life – its successes as well as its failures. Defeat and victory – both are necessary. Flowers and thorns – passing through everything one reaches the temple of existence.

Never ask for anything from existence because there is a contradiction between asking and loving. Love only

gives. And a love which gives all – even one's self –
becomes prayerfulness.

P.S. When I come to Ajmer, come too. Your questions
are such that I will be able to answer them more easily if
you are sitting in front of me, because then, without
anything being said, much is said.

17.

Love.
You are about to enter the temple of love and I am
unable to be present there. This pains my heart, but my
good wishes will certainly be there. You will feel their
presence in the air.
May your life become a life of freedom in the sky of
love. This is my wish to existence.
Many times, in the name of love, dependence sets in,
and love dies. The flowers of love can only bloom in
freedom. So don't let your marriage become a
"marriage." Let it remain love.
How many graves of love have sprung up in the name of
marriage! Do not lay claim to one another, rather, free
one another – because love frees. That which chains is
not love.
My respectful greetings to everyone there.

18.

Love.
Your letters have arrived, filled with your soul's songs,
with their symphonies and music, as if you yourself had
come.
I see you approaching, dancing toward me so you can

disappear in me. Your subtle body has often come close to me in this way. Don't you know this?

You know it, you certainly know it; you know it very well!

Love to everyone there.

19.

Love.

I am extremely happy to have received your letter.

Missing home is natural, and it tortures you until you have learned to turn every place into your home. This art is worth learning.

Now, as long as you are there, live, accepting that place as your home. This whole earth is our home, and all of life is our family.

The rest, when we meet.

Give my regards to everyone there.

20.

Love.

I am very happy to receive your letter.

Life is the name of ever-new experiences. Only one who is capable of experiencing the new every day is alive.

So approach this foreign land lovingly. Learn the new. Make the unfamiliar familiar. Know, become acquainted with, the unknown.

Certainly in all of this you will have to change. Old habits will die, so let them die. And don't be afraid of changing yourself. Change is always good. Inertia is always evil.

And to be always looking toward the past is dangerous because that obstructs the creation of the future.

Life is always ahead of us, not behind. So look ahead,

further and further ahead. Live in dreams, not in memories. Whatsoever is there, don't look at it with condemnation. That way of looking is wrong. Wherever you are, always look for the good, for the beautiful. And the beautiful resides in every place, in every person. All that is needed is the eyes to see it.

Remember that we become what we see: good, if we see good, evil, if we see evil. So don't see evil. It will be good for you to drop that Indian habit. I know there is no evil, only evil vision.

My regards to everyone there.

21.

Love.

I am happy to have received your letters.

1. Religion has nothing to do with birth. Those who say they are related value religion no more than flesh, bones, and marrow.

Religion is the nature of the soul. The soul has neither birth nor death. Therefore seek self-nature. That alone is religion.

Avoid the bondages that are tied to birth – Jainism, Buddhism, Mohammedanism, Christianity. On the path of religiousness, there is no bigger obstacle than religion. Say farewell to religions so that religiousness may enter you. Only religions have names and descriptions. Religiousness is nameless. There is no need to name that which is unique.

2. *Upavas* does not mean fasting. Upavas means being close to yourself. Be close to yourself, certainly, but do

not mistake *upavas* for starvation, otherwise you will only be close to food, but not yourself. Yes, it is possible that sometimes you may completely forget about food because you are absorbed in yourself, but that is a completely different matter. Such moments cannot be preplanned. Such moments only come without any effort from you.

3. Discipline is not a spiritual practice. Even if you practice it, you cannot have it because discipline is an indirect happening. It is the shadow of an awakened intelligence. Awaken, and you will find discipline has come.

If you try to bring in discipline before you have become awakened, you will only bring in repression in the name of discipline. Repression is indulgence doing a headstand. It is nothing but indulgence turned upside down. Don't be deceived by it.

4. Neither an indulgent nor a repressed mind is needed because both are in a state of sleep. What is needed is an awakened mind because an awakened mind is the door to one's isness.

5. Certainly, go to the temple, but not to a brick and concrete one. The real temple is found in the being. The real temple is within. Go there, and you go to the temple.

6. What has knowledge got to do with time? What has liberation got to do with age? Knowledge is beyond time and liberation is eternal, so time and age are no obstacles

to them. Nor is *Kaliyuga*, the age of the darkness, nor *Panchamkal*, the so-called inauspicious hour of the day. If bondage is always possible, so too is liberation.

7. Family members will certainly try to get in your way. People in bondage cannot bear to see anyone out of bondage. But never be angry with them, rather, always take pity on them. They are only worthy of pity. If they call you a fool, enjoy it. Don't become serious. Take all their actions as a play. Keep fearlessly following what you feel to be right and true.

The path of religiousness is not a bed of roses, but the one who has the capacity to tolerate the thorns finally becomes the inheritor of the flowers of eternity.
My regards to everyone there.

22.
Love.
Religion has to be reborn in every age. Bodies – every kind of body – grow old and die. Religious sects are the dead bodies of religion; their souls have left them long ago. Their languages have become out-of-date. This is why they no longer touch the human heart, and their echo is heard no longer in the human soul.

Once Dr. John A. Hutton, while speaking to a gathering of priests, asked, "Why has the preaching of religious leaders become so lifeless and dull?"
When nobody stood up to answer, he answered it himself by saying, "They are all dull because preachers are trying to answer questions that nobody is asking."

Religiousness is eternal but its body should always be contemporary. The body is not eternal, nor can it be – not even the body of religion.

23.

Love.

It is good if politics can become free from religious sects. But it is not good for politics to be free from religiousness. Religiousness is the very heartbeat of life. Politics are nothing more than the circumference of life, and just as the circumference cannot exist without the center, politics cannot be honorable, without religiousness. But yes, dishonorable politics can exist without religiousness. And perhaps that is what politics has been reduced to today.

I have heard…

A successful lawyer, a successful thief, and a successful politician arrived at the gates of heaven at the same time. The three were friends and had met up many times during their lives in many situations, so it was not surprising that they should meet again in death.

Saint Peter asked them, "How many times did you lie in your lives? Speak the truth!"

The thief said, "Three times, sir."

As a punishment, Saint Peter asked him to run around heaven three times.

The lawyer said, "Three hundred times, sir."

The lawyer also was allowed to enter heaven but only after he had run three hundred times around it.

But when Saint Peter turned to the politician, he was missing. The gatekeeper, standing nearby, informed

Saint Peter that he had gone to fetch his bicycle.

24.

Love.

People don't learn from what we say, but only from what we are. Words only reach as far as our ears or, at the most, our minds. But the echo of a person's individuality penetrates to the very core.

Fulton Sheen used to give his talks without looking at any prepared speech. He would deliver the whole talk extemporaneously.

When some friends asked him what his secret was, he replied, "Once an old woman, seeing someone give a talk from a written script, asked in amazement, 'If this man cannot remember his own talk, how does he expect us to be able to remember it?'"

Indeed, we cannot expect others to be what we ourselves are not. And we need not expect others to be what we are because what we are is, by its very nature, infectious.

25.

Love.

Our so-called lives are nothing but sleep. Everything is being done in sleep, otherwise, it would be impossible to do what man does.

It is impossible to create a hell for yourself in an awakened state.

One morning, the preacher in a church saw that a man was deeply asleep.

To let him know that he was sleeping, the preacher said, "All those of you who want to go to heaven, please stand up!"

Everyone, except the sleeping man, stood up.

When everyone had sat down again, the preacher said in a rather loud voice, "Now, all those of you who want to go to hell, please stand up."

Startled, the sleeping man stood up.

But seeing that only he was standing, he said to the preacher, "I don't know what we are voting for, Reverend, but it looks like you and I are in the minority."

26.

Love.

Life is a game of the mind. Happiness–unhappiness, peace–restlessness are all extensions of the mind.

There was a man who used to catch cold during the summer.

A physician checked him and found there was nothing wrong with his body. He advised the patient, "Every day, you should imagine that light from the hot sun is falling on your head, and in this way, even during the winter, you will feel warm, and you won't have to worry about catching a cold."

But in less than a week the man's wife was calling the doctor and requesting in a very nervous voice, "Please come soon. My husband has been taken very ill."

The physician asked, "What is wrong?"

The answer came, "Sitting inside the house he suddenly got sunstroke!"

27.

Love.

Extremes are tension. Non-extremes are relaxation.
But the human mind lives in extremes. Friend or enemy
– but never neutral. Indulger or renouncer – but never
neutral. Either this end or that end – but never in the
middle, as if the mind doesn't know the golden mean at
all! This is the anguish of man. This is man's hell.
Heaven is in the middle – in the middle of two hells – in
the middle of two extremes. Balance is heaven. Balance
is liberation.

A man said to Zen master, Hiki, "My wife is very
miserly; my house has become a hell. Please, do
something for me."
Hiki went to see his wife and showed her his closed fist.
Naturally the woman asked, "What do you mean by this?"
Hiki replied, "Suppose my fist were always like this,
what would you call it?"
The woman laughed and said, "Your hand would be
distorted."
Then, bringing his hand in front of her face, Hiki
opened his fist fully and asked, "And what if it were
always like this?"
The woman laughed again and said, "Another kind of
distortion."
Now it was Hiki's turn to laugh.
He kept laughing and started getting ready to leave.
Then the woman asked, "What does this mean?"
Hiki said, "Now, I have nothing to say. If you
understand this much, you understand everything. All
the scriptures and all the awakened ones say nothing

more than this. Extremes are not allowed because extremes are perversions. Extremes are not your nature. And to be your nature is religiousness."
Hiki went away laughing and the woman was transformed.

That woman was intelligent. Intelligent is the one who can understand such hints. But such intelligent people are so few in the world!

28.
Love.
Theism is not a doctrine. Theism is not theology. Theism is a way of looking at life and living life, a way of looking at beauty and living beauty, a way of looking at truth and living truth, a way of looking at godliness and living godliness.

One day Whitefield said, "Whatever God creates is perfect. His creations have no faults."
Upon hearing this, a hunchback stood up from among the congregation and asked, "What is your opinion of me?"
The question created a pin-drop silence in the church.
"My opinion of you," said Whitefield looking very sympathetically at him, "is that I think God has made a hunchback in whom I see no faults."

29.
Love.
Live each moment. Whatever task comes your way, do it. Do not leave anything for tomorrow. The habit of postponement is suicidal.

Where is tomorrow anyway? What is, is today. What is, is now. This has to be lived. The moment has to be lived. Only the moment is real. He who becomes capable of living the moment, reaches the eternal. The lived moment becomes eternal. Unlived, even eternity is nothing but momentary.

30.

Love.

Drop this fear, because the moment you hold on to fear it increases. To hold on to it is to nourish it. But dropping fear does not mean fighting with it. Fighting too is holding on to it.

Fear *is* – just know this. Do not run away from it. Do not escape from it.

There is fear in life. There is insecurity. There is death. Just know this: that it is so. All this is a fact of life. Where will you run to? How will you escape? This is just the way life is. Its acceptance, its natural acceptance, is freedom from fear. Once fear is accepted, then where is it? Once death is accepted, then where is it? Once insecurity is accepted, then where is it?

Acceptance of the totality of life is what I call sannyas.

31.

Love.

Take the obstacles coming in the way of your resolve as gifts from existence, because without them there will be no way for that resolve to intensify.

For the wise, rocks on the path will become stepping-stones, not obstacles.

In the end, everything depends on you. Nectar can turn

into poison and poison can turn into nectar. Flowers are hidden among the thorns. The one who runs away from thorns unnecessarily misses the flowers. There are diamonds hidden within the mines, but only stones and pebbles will come to hand when you first look for them. If you become disheartened, you will miss finding those diamonds forever.

Every moment is precious. Time never goes back, and opportunities lost become lifetimes missed. When the night is darkest, know that the dawn is near.

32.

Love.

There are many centers in a man's personality, but like a tangled reel of cotton, everything in him has become mixed up. The mind is functioning as the sex center, and because of this, perverted cerebral sex has arisen.

I am reminded of a story…

One of the nobles in Napoleon's court came back early from a journey.

Arriving home he found his wife in the arms of the head priest of the capital.

For a moment, he was taken aback, but then he very gracefully walked to the window and stood there blessing the people outside.

His wife asked him in a nervous tone, "What are you doing?"

He replied, "Monsignor is performing my functions, so I am performing his!"

It isn't right for such things to occur at the center of the mind, but that is what is happening, and naturally, the outcome can be seen everywhere. There is less intelligence, less consciousness, and more insanity. Man has become an insane creature.

For the mind to be healthy, each of its centers should do its own work and not the work of others. When all the mind's centers are rooted in themselves, then man too is rooted in himself. And to be rooted in oneself is to be healthy.

33.

Love.

Dawn is about to break. Now, let go of last night's chattering dreams and prepare to welcome the sun.

The last morning star is disappearing. Forget the past and look forward to the future.

Your prayers have been heard and the doors to the temple of the divine are about to open. Focus on them. Don't let your eyes wander here and there. Don't let your ears hear anything else. Don't let your heart ask for anything else.

Waiting and prayerfulness, prayerfulness and waiting.

34.

Love.

Keep going. The symptoms are good. The Ganges of meditation is still at Gangotri, the source, but it longs to reach the ocean, and the ocean is not far away. If your resolve is total, that Gangotri will reach the ocean.

It is a lack of resolve that creates this distance from the ocean. Gather your resolve, because scattering your resolve lessens it. Just as accumulating sunrays will turn into fire, so accumulating resolve will turn into power. This power is in everyone. This power is an intrinsic right. Awaken it, gather it. Its sleep is the world. Its awakening is ultimate liberation.

35.

Love.

No, nothing is in man's hands because man is a wave in the ocean – inseparable from the ocean.

So, do not think, simply live: in the moment – now and here. And do not compare. Comparing two moments is madness. Moments are atomic. There is no way you can compare one with another.

Living is the only possibility – other than living, there is no way of knowing. Simply know that living is the only knowing. And there only bliss abounds because, except for a comparing mind, there is no lack of bliss anywhere.

36.

Love.

Pour, throw, scatter juice all around. Do not hold on to it, share it – because shared, it will grow. As soon as you stop sharing, it will die.

All the arts have their origin in this compulsion to share juice. Juice, in its eagerness to manifest, becomes art. It becomes a song. It becomes a sculpture. It becomes a Buddha, a Kabir, a Krishna.

Pour, throw, scatter juice. Rising, sitting; sleeping, waking – share it.

Stopped, that juice becomes poison. Shared, it becomes nectar.

37.

Love.

The play of existence is marvelous. My work also happens through opposition, and perhaps it could not happen without it.

That is why I feel only gratitude for those who oppose me. Those who crucified Jesus have not been judged rightly because without them, nobody would have known Jesus. The cross, the foundation on which the temple of Jesus arose was created by his enemies. Alas! Had they but known it. But Jesus certainly knew it. Jesus even said, "They know not what they do."

People like Socrates are not given poison without a reason – they are certainly fit for it – they deserve it because that poison itself becomes the nectar for their messages.

This is why I say the play of existence is marvelous!

38.

Love.

Existence worries about those who stop worrying about themselves. But as long as one *is*, this worrying will not go away. In fact, the existence of "oneself" is the real problem; all other problems are but a pale echo of this basic one.

Ignoring this fundamental source, man wastes his whole life trying to destroy this source's shadows. But like Ravana's heads, before one head has fallen a new one has already grown. We keep fighting with the branches while still watering the roots. Such is the idiocy that is masquerading as man.

But one who has the branches in his hands can also look

for the roots. Don't fight the branches — rather, with their help, go to the depths and seek out the roots. There will be nothing to concern you there. The sense of "I," the ego, will be there, but just seeing it will be enough to make it disappear. It can only live when it is hidden away in darkness.

39.

Love.

There are thorns on the path of truth — not few, but many — but therein the tests of love and truth are found. Those wishing to find the flowers of truth will have to pass through these thorns.

Truth is not cheap. It never was, and it never will be. Pay the price — and don't be afraid. Beyond the crucifix lies the throne.

40.

Love.

Do not mistake the business of daily routines for life. They are necessary in order to live, but they are not life itself. Those who mistake the means for the goal unnecessarily fall from the center of life.

One who cannot be empty, for whom an unoccupied moment becomes burdensome and boring, is simply deceiving himself and preventing himself from seeing himself and the truth. He is not allowing himself to see the futility of his life; he is not allowing himself to see that which is.

To keep sleeping under such self-deception is sick. Only one who can be blissful in unoccupied moments, is healthy. Only one who is not interested in escaping from himself is healthy. Only one who is utterly happy and content with himself is healthy.

So, if anger is there, nothing will come from repenting it. If anger is there, live it, and know it. Go through it – drink its poison and burn in its fire. Experiencing the fire of anger totally will lead to jumping out of it. Repentance and the like are only devices to perpetuate anger. What is achieved after repentance except the very state that was there before the anger – only for anger to happen again?

Repentance is the ego re-establishing itself. Tears of repentance come from the workings of a cunning mind – otherwise, it would be impossible to be angry again, wouldn't it?

The path to heaven inevitably passes through hell. But those who are skilled at closing their eyes find themselves in hell and get stuck there.

Open your eyes – do not deceive yourself. If anger is there, then know that "I am anger." Do not run hither and thither. Stay with the fact. Stay in the fire. Then jump – out of the fire, out of this hell.

But man's cunning mind says: "I am not bad, and if anger comes to me, it comes in spite of me. The evil is not in me. The evil is in the circumstances" or, "The evil is in the other." Understand such cunning. Such cunning is very costly because hell is built on its foundations.

Watch the anger itself. Do not busy yourself with finding causes for it: that will mean you are avoiding seeing the anger. The only thing that can save you from anger is seeing it.

Man is alone – absolutely alone. That is why love is.

That is why prayer is. But this search is bound to fail. It is bound to fail because man cannot find anyone other than himself. Such is his destiny. Such is the law.

That is why the love and prayer that are born out of a passion for seeking the other will always end in suffering. Nobody is at fault when they do this; it is simply their ignorance of the laws of life. But they will have to suffer the consequences of ignoring them.

Yes, there is also another love, there is also another prayer, but they come from searching for and attaining oneself. Then love is not a demand, it is giving. Then, prayer is not a desire, it is the gratitude of a grateful mind.

41.

Love.

It is not I, but existence itself that has accepted you. Am I there? Look – can I be seen anywhere? Having let go of myself, I have become transparent. That is why anyone who has eyes can see right through me.

You have those eyes. Drop your shyness and look – can I be seen anywhere? I cannot. Now, only existence is. And when I say "I" – that too is being said by existence.

So, many times my "I" does not even seem to be humble because it is not mine at all. And for the one whose it is, what humbleness, what ego?

42.

Love.

The indications are very good. The destination is not too far away. Keep moving ahead with prayerfulness. Whatever is happening, whatever experiences are happening, are precious. But do not think about them;

just remain a witness to them. In such a state, thoughts will be a hindrance. Analysis will be fragile.
Interpretation will be destructive. More unique insights will come while you are on the path, but every time, just look at them and keep moving on ahead. You should not stop for them, not even for one moment.
From now on, not stopping for these insights will be your spiritual discipline. Nothing more needs to be done; just be a watcher. These moments are testing.
And, remember: only one in a thousand starts moving in this direction; of those who start moving, only one in a thousand keeps going and from those who keep going, only one in a thousand arrives.
But about you I am completely hopeful.

43.

Love.
Thinking has a hypnotic energy. That is why as you think, so you will become. Sow the seeds of thought very carefully, because as you sow, so will you reap.
If you believe you are uncourageous, you will become so. But remember: you are thinking this not because you are so. On the contrary, you "are" this because you think you are.
Man is what he thinks he is. All forms that we are given are thought projections. That is why, where there is no thought there is no one. That is why, where there is no thought there is only the formless. That is why, where there is no thought there is only the attributeless.
Consciousness without thought is godliness.
If you want to give something a form, give it intelligently, otherwise, don't give anything. If you want to think, be

careful. Otherwise, jump into no thought without a care. If you want to be something, do so thoughtfully. Yes – if you want not to be, then there is no room for thinking. But to be without thinking is dangerous because then forms will become distorted and ugly.

If you cannot search for the truth yet, then at least search for beauty. Then the search for beauty will eventually take you to the search for truth, because truth is the ultimate beauty, and the formless is the perfect form.

44.

Love.

Now, do not delay; drown in meditation. You have already delayed so much. Try to remember that this has been your desire for so many lives. Remember this now – be resolute now. Without courage, life after life will pass you by.

Without resolve, opportunity after opportunity will be uselessly wasted.

Without resolve, life is but a dream.

If there is resolve, even dreams will become realities.

If there is no resolve, even realities will remain dreams.

Resolve is the alchemy that transforms stones and pebbles into diamonds.

45.

Love.

Realizing you are ignorant is a great achievement. It is an essential condition for entering the temple of knowing. Your knowledge is disappearing; that is good. Borrowed knowledge always ends up proving to be futile. If it does not there will only be danger.

Covering up ignorance is not knowledge. Forgetting ignorance is not knowledge, even though that is what people usually call it. And this kind of knowledge will block the doorway for any real knowledge to enter. Throw out such knowledge mercilessly. Throw it out like garbage. And don't keep looking back at it. Move ahead – ahead, where the sun of knowledge is shining – into self-knowledge, into self-experience, into meditation, into enlightenment.

46.

Love.
I will do all that is possible for you, and even that which is not possible, because there is nothing that is impossible. Help is being given to you in many ways, both visible and invisible. You are experiencing it. Slowly, slowly the experience will become even clearer. It takes a little time for the mind to adjust itself to grasping the invisible, but whatever is being experienced, watch it meditatively, with closed eyes. Then slowly, slowly your third eye will be activated.
The senses that have been familiar to you up until now will be of no use in the realms of the invisible, because they have their limitations. Those visions are subtle and nonphysical.
Your first and faint acquaintance with them has begun. This is good, and I am happy.

47.

Love.
Life is a dream, a rainbow stretching between birth and death. It is, and yet it is not. When it is not,

that too makes no difference.

So let go of worrying about the body and search for your self, your consciousness – that which is in the body but is not the body.

As one awakens to that bodilessness everything will be transformed, as if it were midnight and yet the sun were suddenly rising, or as if the Ganges had suddenly appeared in the desert. Everything will be transformed.

So do not waste your time with meaningless worrying or meaningless hopes. Because in life, there is no hope but the soul.

48.

Love.

Mind is like the flame of a lamp flickering in a gust of wind. It will waiver. It will fall into doubt. It will keep being schizophrenic.

You must go beyond it. Distance yourself from it. Rise above it. Leave it behind – leave it below.

You are not the mind. You are only that which knows the mind – knows its trembling, knows its doubting. Stay rooted in this knowing. Stay, and delight in this watchfulness. Simply be this witness. And then, out of this transcendence, the mind will become calm.

Just as when a gust of wind stops, the lamp's flame no longer flickers. Identifying with the mind is like the gusts of wind. When the identification goes, the storms stop. And where there are no storms there is bliss.

49.

Love.

It is not for nothing that Meera sings that the beloved's

bed of love is a cross. It truly is. Or is it that the cross is a bed of love?

But in the bliss of searching for the beloved, one does not worry about crosses. Thorns lying on the path of love suddenly become flowers. There, even darkness becomes light, and poison, nectar.

Unfortunate are those who do not know that such poison is nectar. But you are beginning to know this, and you will come to know it more and more.

And so it is not at all surprising if those who do not know this have become envious of you.

50.

Love.

Sannyas is the greatest rebellion – against the world, against society, against culture. It is a changing of values. It is a revolution within oneself, by oneself, on one's own. That is why all kinds of hardships will have to be endured. There will be opposition. There will be ridicule. Become a witness to all of this. This is the test. And through it you will be refined and will emerge more brightly.

Be grateful to those who harass you because they are providing an opportunity for you to be tested. Endure it all with humility. Accept it all with contentment. Then you will find that no one is an enemy in this world except one's own ego.

51.

Love.

Of course life is a challenge – a multi-dimensional one. That is why life is not static, but dynamic. Endlessly. So those who do not take life as a challenge aren't living at all, they are only dying a slow death. Their whole lives, from birth to death, are only progressing in one direction – toward death. Their destination is fixed, because their goal is death.

Life is uncertain, each moment is new: unplanned, unexpected. There can be no predictions about life. There is no astrology for life. All astrology is about death. That is precisely why life is a challenge and death is a rest.

Life is a struggle, but death is only a rest for those who have gone through the struggle of life. For those who did not live, death brings nothing but fear. For one who is alive, death simply does not exist. It is out of the struggles of life that a restful death is earned. It is earned through living.

Therefore, the one who dies a death that is earned attains deathlessness. Like a Jesus, like a Socrates. Earn death – that is the only essential challenge of life.

52.

Love.

Do not be afraid. Let whatsoever is happening in meditation happen.

If the mind is catharting do not stop it. This is the only way for it to be purified. Whatsoever is suppressed in the unconscious will surface. Give it passage, so that you can be free from it. The moment you repress it, meditation will be wasted. And no sooner will you be free from it than meditation will be realized.

So welcome each thing that comes up, even help it, because the work that takes a long time on its own is accomplished in a short time if there is help.

53.

Love.

You are accepted – you are accepted forever, just as you are.

The doors of the temple of existence are always open, unconditionally. No one – except the person who is not able to accept himself – is rejected in the temple of existence.

But the responsibility for non-acceptance is ours alone. Self-condemnation is irreligious – perhaps the only irreligiousness. Self-condemnation is the only original sin, because the person who condemns himself will be unable to offer himself to existence.

In life, only the flower that blooms by totally accepting itself can be offered at the feet of the divine.

P.S. Love to Soodji. How is his health now? Taking care of him is your *sadhana*, your meditation.

54.

Love.

Attaining meditation is not a question of *time*. It is one of will.

If the will is total, meditation can happen in any moment. But a mind without will can wander for life after life. Intensify the will. Crystallize the will. Totalize the will. Then meditation will knock at your door of its own accord.

Your mind will certainly torture you as long as there is no meditation. Mind is nothing but the name for an absence of meditation. Just as darkness is the name for an absence of light – just the same.

As light comes, the darkness will disappear.

As meditation comes, the mind will go away. So immerse yourself in meditation now. All else will follow it of its own accord.

55.

Love.

Why do you become hopeless? Isn't hopelessness just the result of extreme hope? Why do you become sad? Isn't sadness just the shadow of extreme expectation? If hopelessness is total, it leaves no room for further hopelessness. If sadness is total, even sadness turns into celebration.

That is why I say: Drop all duality. Drop all games of light and shadow. Wake up, and know that that which is – is. If there is darkness, then there is darkness. If there is death, then there is death. If there is poison, then there is poison. And then look: Where is darkness? Then search: Where is death?

Darkness is found in the desire for light. Death is found in the endless lust for life. And poison is nothing but a demand for the elixir of immortality.

56.

Love.

The world is neither misery nor happiness.

What we are seeking becomes the world. Our outlook becomes our world. Each one of us is the creator of his own world. If each moment of life brings you misery, then somewhere or other there is a fault in your outlook. And if all that you can see is darkness all around, then you have certainly closed the same eyes that can see light. Think about yourself again. Look at yourself afresh. If you blame others, you will not be able to seek out your own mistakes. If you blame the circumstances, you will not be able to fathom the roots of your own mental standpoint.

That is why, whatever circumstances you find yourself in, always start by looking for the causes within yourself. The causes are always found within oneself. But they always appear to be in others. If you avoid this misunderstanding it will be difficult to hold on to misery. Others simply function as mirrors. The face is always our own.

Life can be a big celebration, but we need to recreate ourselves anew. That work is not difficult, because the moment we see the folly of our own outlook, that folly begins to die and a new man starts to be born.

57.

Love.

Sannyas is the musical chorus of all that is good, beautiful, and true in life.

Without sannyas there is no fragrance in life. Life, by itself, is nothing more than roots. As long as the flower of sannyas does not bloom, life will not reach meaning, bliss, and gratitude.

I am extremely happy to know that this precious moment of self-revolution has arrived in your life. I have seen that moment in your eyes. Just as at dawn, before the sun rises, the sky is filled with reddish hues, I have seen those daybreak colors spreading over your heart. Birds are singing a song of welcome and dormant plants are awakening. It is not right to delay anymore. Isn't it late enough already?

58.

Love.

Except for surrender – total let-go – there just is no way to reach the temple of godliness.

Leave – leave everything to that. Don't carry an unnecessary burden on your head. "Whatever life wants" – keep this sutra forever in your remembrance. Jesus has said: "Thy will be done." Keep saying this to yourself. Let it begin to reverberate all the way from the conscious to the unconscious.

Awake or asleep, let this tune start to play within you, and then, at any moment, as your let-go becomes total, enlightenment will happen. The end of let-go is enlightenment. The dispersal of oneself is let-go. Say: "Whatever life wants" and look within.

Don't you see something crumbling and disappearing? Don't you see something new and unfamiliar being born?

59.

Love.

Do not fight with yourself. It is futile because no victory is ever achieved through such a fight. Fighting with yourself is nothing but a gradual suicide.

Accept yourself, joyfully, gratefully. All that is, is good. Sex too, anger too, because whatever is, comes from existence. Accept it, and understand it. Seek out, and unravel, the hidden possibilities within it.

Then even sex will be seen as a seed of godliness, and anger will become the door to forgiveness. Evil is not an enemy of the good. Rather, evil is simply good that has been blocked.

60.

Love.

The world is a dream, a dream seen with open eyes.
What is between birth and death is not the truth,
because truth has neither birth nor death. All births are a
dream; all deaths also are a dream. That which has a
beginning and an end is a dream. That which has no
beginning and no end is the truth.

Without seeking out such truth, life is futile – and the
interesting thing is that this truth is within oneself. You
don't have to go anywhere to look for it – neither to Kashi
nor to Kaaba. You don't have to wait for the future or for
an opportunity to search for it. It is available now and here.
But man looks for it everywhere in search of it except
within himself. He searches everywhere but within
himself. As a result, he reaches everywhere except
himself, and at the cost of losing himself, he finds
everything else. In this way, the one who could have
become an emperor becomes a beggar through his own
doing. Don't fall into such falsehood anymore.

Go deeply into meditation so that you may know the
truth of yourself. Understand the dream of this world so
that you may know the truth of yourself. Search for that
which is unborn and unknown so that you can find
that which is immortal.

61.

Love.

Strive for meditation, and all problems of the mind will
disappear.

In fact, mind is the problem. All the rest of the problems
are only echoes of the mind. To fight with each problem

separately will solve nothing. Fighting with echoes is futile. There will be no outcome except defeat. Do not prune the branches, because in place of one branch four will grow. When you prune branches, trees grow even more. The problem is in the branches.

If you are going to cut something, then cut the roots, because by cutting the roots, the branches will disappear on their own.

Mind is the root. Cut this root with meditation. Mind is the problem. Meditation is the solution. There is no solution in the mind. There is no problem in meditation because there is no meditation in mind, and there is no mind in meditation.

The absence of meditation is mind. The absence of mind is meditation. That is why I say: Strive for meditation.

62.

Love.

I am always with you.

Whenever you are wavering in your meditation, remember me, and you will find help has arrived through invisible hands. The forces that can be seen are not the only ones. In truth, they are nothing but tiny streams behind which lies an ocean of invisible forces, and their source too is in the invisible.

But, to take help from the invisible is an art, perhaps the highest art. Leaving oneself silently, helplessly, in the hands of the invisible, a connection is made with the vastness of the beyond.

Right now, I am only functioning as a ladder in between. The moment you establish direct contact you will have to leave the ladder behind. One has to go up the ladder but then get off it as well.

At present you remember me, but later you will forget me. But only the one who has remembered in the first place will be able to forget!

63.

Love.

If only you were unworthy, it would be easy to make you worthy.

Where is the difficulty in awakening the sleeping? But the difficulty in awakening the awakened is great! Isn't it? No one is unworthy – that is the difficulty. No one is undeserving – that is the difficulty. Godliness is present in each and every iota of the universe, so *what* unworthiness? Only godliness is, nothing else is; so where is this undeserving-ness?

Therefore, only remember your self. Remember. Remember. And, remember that I am always by your side. Not in the house – I am present in your very heart. Close your eyes and see. Am I not there?

64.

Love.

Fruit has begun to appear on the tree of meditation. Dance, rejoice, and thank existence. A thirst of lifetimes is about to be quenched. What you have always desired is about to happen. Do not be afraid, no matter what happens.

Remain a blissful witness, even if death seems to be happening, because enlightenment is beyond the death that happens in meditation. Enlightenment is deathless. From now on it will be a steep climb because the summit is close. But go on moving forward patiently and prayerfully. Whenever you get entangled, or the path seems to be lost, or you start losing courage, or doubt overtakes you, remember me immediately. But as far as possible, don't call me about everyday matters. Wrestle with these situations yourself. Fight them out for yourself. When there is no other means and you find you are helpless, only then remember me. Although, even without your call, I will keep doing whatever is necessary.

65.

Love.

Do not worry.

In life, there is no such thing as worry. Understand that everything is a dream. Indeed it is. That which is today and is not tomorrow is nothing but a dream.

Don't immerse yourself too much in it. Worry is born out of this immersion. Come out of the dream. Distance yourself a little, and then look at things. Become a bit of a watcher.

To immerse yourself in a dream is to suffer, and to wake up while dreaming breaks the dream. And that, in itself, is bliss.

66.

Love.

Life is indeed incomplete without godliness.

That is why it feels incomplete to you. However, this awareness of emptiness, this realization of incompleteness is fortunate, because from this realization and because of this realization, *Athato brahman jigyasa:* now the inquiry into the ultimate begins.

Just don't avoid such awareness, don't run away from such emptiness, don't escape from such a realization, even though the mind will only suggest escaping, and that escape is the world.

The world is an escape. The entire busy-ness of the world is an escape; a futile effort to fill the emptiness. So nothing but anguish will result from this race.

What is needed is godliness, but we fill that emptiness with things. What is needed is religiousness, but we fill it with money. What is needed is the self, but we fill it with the other. Then everything is attained and yet nothing is attained. Then the emptiness becomes more and more intense.

Precious are such moments because they are the moments for choosing and deciding.

So you can either choose escape or choose not to escape. If you choose to escape, then there will be the usual outcome. For lifetime upon lifetime there has always been the same outcome.

Stop now, and don't choose escape. Don't run away from emptiness – rather settle in emptiness. Don't fill up the emptiness, rather allow the emptiness to fill *you* up completely. Then that transformation which is called sannyas will happen. And you will reach that point where all emptiness has dissipated.

But remember, this does not happen intellectually. Don't think: know now, experience now.

Haven't you already thought and pondered enough?

67.
Love.
Don't hurry.

Be patient. Patience feeds the soil of meditation. Keep nurturing meditation. The fruit is bound to come. It always comes. Don't worry about the fruit, because your very worrying will hinder its coming.

That very worrying will distract you from meditation. Meditation demands your whole attention. A divided being won't do. Partiality won't do. Meditation is not possible without your totality.

So focus on the act of meditation, and leave the fruit of meditation to the hands of existence. That fruit will come, because total immersion in meditation gives birth to it.

68.

Love.

I see – I am seeing – your mind: blowing now hot, now cold. Your feet faltering on the path; again and again losing and finding it – I am watching all of this.

I feel compassion. Whatever I can do, whatever can be done, I am doing. And yet, I cannot hasten things because every seed takes its own time to sprout. To wait for that is a must.

What is more, the human mind can busy itself trying to manage two contradictory possibilities simultaneously, and then the situation will become even more complex. Can't you yourself see that you have boarded two boats at the same time?

69.

Love.

Life is not divided – neither in time, nor space.

If life is anything, it is undividedness – an uninterrupted

flow. Past, present, and future are lines drawn by man on the uninterrupted flow of time. In reality, they exist nowhere but in man's mind. Mind is time.

Space is also undivided. I do not end at my body – in fact, my boundary is the boundlessness of the whole. But the mind cannot rest without dividing. It is like a prism: dividing is its very nature. Passing through the mind, the ray of existence gets divided into many different rays and colors.

That which is one at the root becomes many in the branches. The root is eternal – beginningless and endless. Branches are temporal – they have an end as well as a beginning. Branches change. Roots are permanent. Roots neither change nor can be changed. Yes, change can be desired, but then such a desire inevitably leads you into failure and anguish. Branches go on changing. You cannot stop them changing. But a non-changing state can certainly be desired, and then such a desire will inevitably lead to failure and anguish. The West is in the first kind of failure and anguish. The East is in the second kind of failure and anguish.

Up until now, man has not been able to bring about a culture that not only succeeds but also bears fruit. Only when there is a harmonious balance between the two truths that I have been talking about – the truth of the roots and the truth of the branches, the law of the permanent and the law of the changing – can a culture which is not polarized and one-sided, which uses the tension of opposing polarities like architects do when building arched brick doorways, come into being.

The truth of life is *anekant*, multiplicity. The current of life always flows between two banks of opposite polarity.

70.

Love.
Closeness and distance are all dreams. Truth is oneness.
That is why even when you are very close, there is no
closeness, and even when you are far away, there is no
distance. Everything is happening in a dream – and yet
nothing is happening, and that is why it is a dream.
Now, break the dream. You have seen many dreams –
life after life. Now, wake up. You have seen happiness –
you have seen sorrow. You have had births – you have
had deaths, but now, wake up in life. Now, settle in bliss.
Let go of closeness; let go of distance.
Now, seek unity, oneness.

71.

Love.
I am in bliss to know that you are in bliss.
Bliss is your self-nature; that is why you long for it.
Unhappiness is anti-nature. It is a fall from the self. That
is why you are trying to free yourself from it.
The pain is not being who we are. The tension is not
being what we are. The moment you settle into yourself,
there is health. The moment you come back to
yourself, there is peace.
Wandering is on the circumference. You settle at the
center. You have had your first glimpse of settling. The
first ray from your center has touched you. Now, you
will have to move even more deeply – because only when
even the center of the self is lost will the total depth of
the self be found.

72.

Love.

Today is enough for living.

To worry about what will be coming tomorrow is enough to destroy today. If sects are going to form, then the people who are going to destroy them will also be born. Are destroyers like me to stop their work completely?

One has to build and one has to destroy. One has to destroy and one has to build. And those able to see both as two sides of the same coin become free from both. Dead truths are called tradition, but that which is born also has to die. You cannot stop children being born because you fear that tomorrow a grave will need to be dug for them. Just because corpses were once alive doesn't mean they are now. Birth will continue, but death will also continue.

A religion is born, but when it dies it becomes a sect. Sects have to go to their graveyards. Religion will be born again, and again a sect will form. Those who are fighting for the birth of a religion are those who will eventually give birth to new sects. And those who give rebirth to a religion will have to take part in the drama of fighting their own kind.

The Upanishads pretend to fight the Vedas. That is why their name is vedant, meaning the one who brings the Vedas to an end. How ironic! It is the Vedas that they reestablish and it is the Vedas that they fight against. Buddha fights against the Upanishads – and there is no greater Vedantin than Buddha. Shankara fights Buddha; and who is a greater Buddhist than Shankara?

73.

Love.

If love is there, there are no questions because love is always ready to lose everything.

But if there is no love, then there are only questions and more questions. If this is the case, then consolations and such things will be needed.

Love is mad, or blind. But the madness of love has infinitely more blessings than being sensible with no love. And it is infinitely more worthwhile to embrace the blindness of love than to embrace eyes with no love.

But love is there when it is there, and not when it is not. One should understand clearly whether such madness, such blindness, is there or not. Because if there is no love but only madness, no love but only blindness, then one should listen carefully to society – because in such situations, society will eventually prove to be right.

And remember that love never falls into thinking about such things.

If love is anything, it is risk. It is offering oneself into the hands of the unknown. Love is a leap into insecurity. Society is a security system. That is why struggle is natural. But that struggle is not, as it seems to be, between oneself and society. The struggle is between one's own security and insecurity.

If there is love, then where is society? If there is no love, then what else but society exists?

74.

Love.

Keep showering in the water of meditation. The flower of sannyas is bound to bloom. But a constant effort is needed. The echo of meditation has to resound in your each and every heartbeat.

Sannyas is easy, but not cheap. And the reason it is not cheap is because it is easy. To attain the simple is the hardest thing in life.

Meera has said: "The plant of love grew because I showered it with my tears." For Meera, love is meditation. For you, meditation will be love. However, both are two poles of one reality.

75.

Love.

The source of failure does not lie within it. That is why, despite trying to kill it again and again, man has been unable to kill failure. And that is why you will not be able to do so either.

You must have read stories where a demon hides his life within a parrot or some other animal, and then the demon can only be killed when the bird or the animal hiding his life away is killed first.

Failure is protected in the same way. Its life is not found within it. Its life is found within the longing for success. That is why whoever wants success cannot be freed from failure – because only those who become free from success itself become free from failure.

You have written that your inferiority complex is increasing because of your failures. No, my brother! Your analysis has harnessed the bullock behind the cart. Inferiority does not increase because of failures; on the contrary, because you feel inferior you want success. That becomes the failure.

But why do you feel inferior? Everyone is as he is:

unique, matchless, incomparable. Comparison is impossible, but comparison is what is being taught. Comparison is your conditioning. Understand this misguided, wrong, dangerous, and ignorant conditioning because to know the wrong as wrong is to become free from it.

76.

Love.

The ocean is one. And so the waves, that seem to be many, cannot be many either.

Within each wave is that same ocean. Only that comes in, only that goes out. The waves are seen because they are the ocean's footprints, its comings and goings. But the waves, quite simply, are not.

Only the ocean is, but it is the waves that are seen, while the ocean remains unseen.

Words are seen, but the truth is not. Bodies are seen, but isness is not.

77.

Love.

The ocean takes care of the waves, and the waves are forever carefree. The sky takes care of the stars, and the stars are forever blissful.

But man worries: he drowns in misery, he is overshadowed by anguish, because he falls into the madness of taking care of himself by himself.

78.

Love.

To lose oneself is to attain all. But that losing should be

total, because if even part of the self is retained, all is retained. It is either nothing, or everything.

There is no middle way. For the self, there is no middle way.

79.

Love.

When the world becomes a blissful play, sannyas happens.

A worldly man lives by dragging the world along like a burden. To know the world as just a play is sannyas.

Sannyas is not opposed to the world; rather it is transforming your attitude toward the world.

And everything – happiness and misery, attachment and aversion, fame and oblivion – everything changes the moment our attitude changes. Our attitude, our very manner of looking at the world, shapes our lives.

Nor is sannyas an argument or theory. In my view, arguing, theorizing, happen when we aren't looking at the world with the eyes of sannyas.

Sannyas is nothing but ultimate juice, ultimate enjoyment, because sannyas means becoming a co-participant with existence. Many times, our very attachment to rocks and pebbles doesn't allow us to reach the diamond mines.

But I will not leave you. The diamond mine is close by, and you have to reach it.

80.

Love.

Perhaps you simply have no idea about juice.

But even if there is only thirst, that is enough. Where in the body will you find this juice? Only its reflection is there. Juice is found in the soul. Or it may be better to say, the soul is juice. It is the echo of this juice that is heard in the body. Catch hold of this echo and search for its source. Otherwise, the body will gradually become frail and infirm, and then the echo will not be heard.

This, alone, is the suffering of the body. This, alone, is the pain of indulgence. This, alone, is the anguish of the senses. This is why the real juice must be found while there is still time, while there is still energy, otherwise, later, nothing but regrets will remain. For, as you say, "What is the point of getting upset when the birds have already eaten the crops"?

81.

Love.

There will be no waiting. How can there be waiting at the very gates of existence?

But for now, waiting is necessary: for your sake, waiting is necessary. You would not be able to tolerate sudden bliss or a sudden upsurge of energy. That is why time is needed. Every phenomenon requires time. A seed takes time to break open. A sprout takes time to appear. A tree takes time to become a tree, and its fruit takes time to grow. And even then, the fruit takes time to ripen.

Only that which happens in its own time is auspicious.

82.

Love.

We do not know life at all; that is why we get bored. We turn life into something mechanical; that is why we get bored.

The way we live life – just dragging along – is why we get bored. There is no boredom in life itself, it comes from our fear of living. We are not only afraid of death, we are afraid of life too!

In reality, we fear death only because we fear life. Death is not an end of life – it is life's culmination. That is why I say: Live, live fearlessly. Say goodbye to the past. Man keeps holding on to it out of fear. Do not invite future dreams; you keep planning to live in the future because you want to avoid living today.

Live today, now and here. Both what is coming and what has passed are deceptions. Only this moment is true. Only this moment is eternal.

83.

Love.

To be mad for the divine is an art. It is a methodical madness.

So become mad, certainly – but do not forget the method. It is the method which I call meditation. Meera calls it love, Mahavira calls it austerity.

No matter what name you give – just don't forget it. The mind wants to forget it. After all, it is death to the mind. And do you know what the easiest, but the most cunning technique the mind has to forget about meditation? To *think about* meditation.

So, remember, that you are not going to think about meditation, you are going to do it.

84.

Love.

Life is a mystery. It can be lived, and it can be known by

living but it cannot be solved like a mathematical problem.

It is not a problem – it is a challenge. It is not a question – it is an adventure. That is why those who only keep asking questions about life remain deprived of answers forever – and it is their own doing. Or they find answers that are not answers. Such answers can be found in the scriptures.

In fact, no answer received from another can be an answer, because the truth of life cannot be borrowed. Or the questioners make up their own answers. In this way, of course, they find consolation, but not solutions, because made-up answers are no answers at all.

Only answers that are known can be answers. That is why I say: Don't ask – live and know. This alone is the difference between philosophy and religiousness: philosophy is asking, religiousness is living. And, the interesting thing is that philosophy certainly asks but never finds the answer, and religion doesn't ask at all, and yet finds it.

85.

Love.

The music of love, of reverence, should echo in every heart.

The temple of man's heart is lying empty and void. There is nothing there except the ashes of logic. And the heart is not a grate that delights in the ash. The heart needs flowers of love, of prayer, of godliness. The heart needs the music of the being, of the invisible, of the immortal. The heart needs to quench its thirst by drinking in light, bliss, and gratitude.

Go to the thirsty. Sing – and shower prayerfulness upon their hearts. Dance – and invite and include them in your dance. Let Meera be reborn in you. That alone is your destiny.

For that alone I have given you the call.

My love to the doctor.

86.

Love.

I will come, I will even come in your sleep. After all, your sleep has to be broken. I will enter your dreams, because you are going to be freed from those dreams.

But is what you call your waking state really that, or is it just another form of sleep? Being awake does not just mean that your eyes are open. If only it were that easy to be awake! Dreams do not cease just because your eyes are open. Our waking state is usually just the illusion of being awake, and our so-called thinking is only our dreams translated into words.

But if you recognize this sleep, you will begin to wake up. And if you become conscious of these dreams, they will begin to cease.

Where there is no dream, where there is no sleep, there is no illusion. And where there is no illusion, that, just that, is what we are seeking.

87.

Love.

Do not waste time on philosophy. The solution is found in the depths of existence.

The waves of thoughts do not go deeper than the surface. Diamonds are found in the depths of the ocean, so one who seeks them in the foam of the waves is seeking in vain.

Philosophy is nothing but the foam that rises up on the waves of our thoughts. Of course, when that foam is shimmering in the sun's rays it can appear to be very beautiful, but it is still only foam and will disappear the moment you take it in your hand.

That is why I say: Meditation is the door – not thinking; emptiness is the door – not words.

Do not ask why existence is. Search for what existence is.

88.

Love.

The path to the temple of godliness is found after lifetimes of seeking, but many times we lose the path even after having found it.

Today, you are standing at the gate to that very path. Now, do not go astray. Resolve to keep moving ahead. Many enticements will stop you, many conditionings will stop you. Laziness will stop you. The mind will suggest other alternatives. Beware of all of these things because the gate you have been seeking for lifetimes can be lost within moments.

A fear of the unknown will surround you. Stepping into the unknown, you will feel insecure, but gather courage and embrace the unknown because this unfamiliarity, this unknown, is itself the gate.

89.

Love.

Love is always without cause.

That is why love that has a cause is love no longer. Love

is not a deal. It is beyond the business world of bargains
– and that is its beauty.

On this material earth, love is a ray of the immaterial.
That is why one can reach prayerfulness through love,
and godliness through prayerfulness.

That is why I say there is no other religion than love.

90.

Love.

Doctrines, ultimately, have no value. Value is found in
experiences. Often, doctrines will hinder you from
entering into an experience, because doctrines close your
consciousness.

Consciousness needs to be open, free, eager for the new.
Consciousness needs to welcome the unknown; to be
eagerly ready to embrace the unknown, unfamiliar truth.
I am pleased to know that you do have such a
consciousness. It is a great treasure and an essential
provision for the journey of a seeker of truth. Neither is
truth found in *isms* – nor can it be. Truth and scripture
never, ever, meet. *Isms* are too narrow. Scriptures are too
limited.

And where is the space for truth in words?

91.

Love.

There is neither birth nor death. There is only life,
beginningless, endless.

Life is there before birth, otherwise, who will be born? It
is also there after death, otherwise, who will have died?
Birth is not the beginning of life, and death is not the end
of life. Birth and death are events that happen within life.

Just as water bubbles form and burst in a river, so too man's bubble forms and bursts within life. The name of this bubble is ego – and certainly, it is born and it dies. Ego is the name of what happens between birth and death.

That is why one who has an ego remains unacquainted with life. If you want to know life, you have to awaken from the ego.

The bubble has simply forgotten that it is not, that only the river is.

92.

Love.

Whenever there is a need, call me, and I will come.

Now, this is no longer just a physical relationship, there is a direct relationship of the soul. At first, it will be in your dreams, and then I will be seen when your eyes are open, when you are awake as well.

But do not call without reason. Neither call out of curiosity or for material reasons.

When a needle can do the work, a sword should not be used, should it?

93.

Love.

That which can be understood is not love.

What is more, understanding is not everything. There is much beyond understanding. That which is beyond understanding is deep. Understanding is on the surface. Understanding is always superficial.

That is why no one is more foolish than the person who stops at understanding. Waves can be understood, but the ocean is beyond understanding.

So understand, certainly, but do not take understanding to be your end. Keep looking beyond it as well. Keep transcending it. It is the transcendence of understanding that eventually becomes the understanding of truth.

94.

Love.

After surrendering oneself into the hands of existence, there is nothing left to be done. Then it is as if everything has started happening by itself.

Rejoice that this is now beginning to happen in your life. Swimming has dropped and floating has begun. I call this state of being, sannyas. The river goes on taking you to the ocean – so why swim? Why make an effort? Why try?

There is grace in this effortlessness, but this does not mean inactivity. Floating too is an activity. But while floating, the doer is absent. When there is action, but no doer, then that is inaction. But when there is no action, and the doer still is, that is not inaction.

Inaction is action that is offered up to existence.

95.

Love.

One cannot raise one's inner strength by oneself. It is like someone trying to lift himself up by his shoelaces. Inner strength grows through surrendering to existence. Except surrender, there is no other door to strength. Except disappearing, there is no other way of reaching. The seed disappears and becomes a tree. The being manifests when the ego dies. Ego is weakness; being is strength. The word *self-strength* is not right; the self itself is the strength.

96.

Love.

One who lives for some purpose always goes astray. His life becomes a burden. This is because purpose is always for tomorrow and living is in the now.

Do not nurture unnecessary tensions. Do not feed unnecessary discord. Do not try to create the present from the future, because that is just not possible. Let the future come out of the present. It comes about so spontaneously, that you will have nothing to do.

Simply live, today. To live, today is enough.

Newman has sung:

> *...I do not ask to see*
> *The distant scene — one step enough for me.*

Yes, of course, today is never right for dying. Tomorrow is needed for dying! That is why those who live for tomorrow don't live; they only die.

Live today — now, wholly, totally. Tomorrow will take care of itself.

97.

Love.

As well as the eyes we can see, there are other eyes. And through them I saw you. As well as the ears we can see, there are other ears. And through them I heard you.

I have touched you, not with the body, but with the heart. If you move into meditation, you will be able to understand all of this. Existence too is beyond senses — infinite, beginningless, endless. Godliness is a collective name for all of this. That is the journey I would like you to embark on.

Come prepared, because, in the end, there is no other reason to come to me.

98.

Love.

Keep moving on ahead, don't be afraid! I am with you. Existence is with you.

What is more, your mind is pure and innocent, and the moment when meditation is going to explode in you is getting close. Whatever is happening inside – all of that is preparing you for that moment. What appear to be obstacles are not obstacles. They are tests. The rocks one encounters on the path are not enemies, they are friends. They can be turned into stepping-stones. They are on the path in order to become stepping-stones.

And then, if needed, I will push you as well! But leave all that to me. You need not concern yourself with that.

99.

Love.

Society is only a combination of people. That is why, in the end, fundamentally, society is only a reflection of people's minds.

If the individual mind is restless, society cannot be peaceful. Only when the individual mind changes will society be peaceful. There is no other alternative. Neither is there any shortcut.

Meditation is the technique for individual transformation. Only when more and more people are moving into meditation can something happen. Only when more and more people enter bliss can something happen.

Taking shelter within existence is the only way.

100.

Love.

The remembrance of everyone stays with me – it does not come. If it were not always there, it would have to come back, and in coming, there would be pain because in coming, going is also hidden.

In remaining, there is bliss. Then there is no coming and no going.

Perhaps, you may not grasp this. I also would not have grasped it if someone had said it to me. There is so much which is simply not understood by trying to understand. On the contrary, it gets even more entangled.

I am saying things as they are. I never remember anybody, and yet remembrance remains. It is like heartbeats: whether I notice them or not, the heart goes on beating. Or like breath: whether I deliberately breathe or not, the breathing continues. Just so is my remembrance.

That is why, when someone asks, "Do you ever remember me or not?" I am in trouble. I think, "What should I say now?" Yes is not right. No is also not right. That is why I laugh and become silent.

But *you* have asked me in writing, not even leaving me the possibility of laughing and remaining silent.

101.

Love.

A whole year has passed, and then somehow you

gathered courage to write a letter?

I called you in your dreams. You certainly heard it, but haven't you understood it yet? The call was given to wake you up. The call was given to break your slumber. Now, rise and walk. If you don't walk, the destination will be very far away. If you walk, it will be very close. Not even close – because closeness is also a distance. In reality, you are the destination. Walk, and find yourself.

102.

Love.

A barber from Baghdad was in great difficulty. Everybody visiting his shop would talk of a beautiful princess whom a magician had imprisoned in a castle. He heard that whoever succeeded in freeing the princess would not only win her hand, but also inherit her entire kingdom.

Yet freeing the princess had proved to be an extremely difficult task. The castle was located deep inside a dense forest. Ninety-nine out of a hundred liberators had been devoured by wild animals. The castle was situated high on a mountain, and ninety-nine out of the hundred who had survived the wild animals had died from being crushed beneath the rocks that demons had rolled down the mountainside. And then those who had managed to survive the demons had been burned to ashes when a fire had suddenly flared up just as they went through the castle door.

A few lucky ones had crossed the forest. A few of them had even gone past the demons, but so far, no one had succeeded in going through the door.

Finally, the barber could endure it no longer. For isn't there a limit to a man's patience? He sold everything he had and set off in search of the beautiful princess.

But, to his surprise, he did not come across any wild animals in the forest. He gave thanks and went on ahead. And amazingly, the demons who used to roll rocks down the mountainside were nowhere to be seen. Filled with hope and longing, he began to run quickly toward the castle. He passed through the doorway – and amazingly, no fire flared up! Bowing his head, he began to give thanks again and again.

Right in front of him stood the throne – and on that throne sat the princess he had heard stories about since his childhood. Fearfully he went forward – but then the castle began to resound with laughter and a voice said, "Now don't be afraid, because what is there to find now, anyway?"

He was standing right in front of the throne, but there was no beautiful young woman sitting there. Instead, there was an old woman, and she was dead. He had completely forgotten that he had been listening to that story for at least sixty years!

103.

Love.

Self, universal self, or *no-self* – Jaina, Hindu or Buddhist – all words only express a partial truth.

Truth can never be expressed in its totality because words are too small and narrow to do this. So don't get entangled with words; whatever feels right to you, whatever appeals to you, just choose that. Not choosing a single word won't hinder your spiritual path – in fact, the hindrance is in the emphasis on words. To Jews, the word for God is Yahweh or Yahoba, which means no name, or nameless.

The search for truth does not even have a distant relationship with theories, scriptures, and doctrines. So it will be better to avoid the scriptures; otherwise, you will lose what you are seeking.

Focus on witnessing – whether it is thoughts or feelings, actions or reactions. Become a witness to all of them.

Don't let the stream of your life be unconscious.

Meditate on awareness. Awareness is meditation.

Leave all the rest to existence or Yahweh – who has no name.

I will not answer your one remaining question because it is useless as far as your path is concerned. Not that the question is wrong, nor, even, that there is no answer to it, just because it is irrelevant to a seeker of truth.

104.

Love.

Seek truth, certainly. But only one who disappears while seeking and searching is able to find truth.

The truth can only appear in its totality when there is a total absence of one's self. Doesn't truth need an inner space to manifest in? Create that space within yourself. If you remain full of yourself, to where can truth come?

Be empty. Be void. Then the ocean of truth will spontaneously fill that void.

Kabir has sung, "Seeking and searching, Oh my beloved friend, Kabir himself disappeared."

That is why I say: "Only those who have lost themselves attain truth."

105.

Love.

Life is illogical. That is why only dead things are found by grasping logic. Life is a mystery. So it inevitably breaks all the boundaries of thinking. Life is also polar. What is born also dies. That is why it is impossible for the one who wants to avoid death to be born.

Religions are born and they die. Institutions are born and they rot away. But that is their destiny; within time and space, that is the destiny of everything.

So bury the old and go on giving birth to the new. There is no way other than this. Certainly, what is new today will become old tomorrow. Then that too will be buried. It is not right to prevent children from being born just because one day they will become old. Nor is it right to prevent the old from being buried just because they were once children.

106.

Love.

What you are searching for can certainly be found. The river finds the ocean. Thirst finds a lake. Prayerfulness finds godliness.

Godliness is close by, but we are not thirsty. Awaken your thirst.

Just become thirst. Then there will not be even one moment's delay in finding it.

107.

Love.

You are seeing darkness, aren't you? See it in its totality. Just don't run away from it. Live in it, wake up in it.

You are running away and you are getting tired.
Escaping from darkness will not bring light, only a deeper darkness. It is not a question of darkness at all. It is a question of being asleep.

Wake up, and the darkness will be gone. Waking up is light.

So wake up: make the darkness itself an object – and wake up. Meditate on the darkness – and wake up.

108.

Love.

If one does not gather courage, one will have to return. There is no question about that at all.

Ah! The same thing happened before, but there you are, sitting there, completely forgetting it.

What a sweet poison forgetfulness is!

109.

Love.

Society cannot be changed directly, because society is only a lifeless structure, a statistical combination of interrelating individuals.

Only individuals can be transformed, because only individuals have a consciousness that can transform itself. And a transformation that does not happen by itself is no transformation at all.

Imposed transformations do not endure, nor will they ever. Man has tried that kind of unscientific endeavor many times, and the result has always been failure.

The individual is the basic unit. Every effort has to be focused only on him. And this has the advantage of everyone being able to start with himself. Whenever things begin with the other, it is violence, no matter how nonviolent it may appear to be at the beginning.

That is why I always say: Leave society and take hold of yourself, because other than that, there is no way to change society.

110.

Love.

Experiences will deepen.

Just try – wholeheartedly, determinedly. If you take a step toward godliness, then even if it is a wrong step, it will never go to waste! The question of a right step doesn't even arise. Walk and see.

Religion means experimenting, not just having faith. Religion is experiencing, not just belief.

111.

Love.

In the same way that the ocean calls the river, I have called you. This is the call that is resonating in your being. It can resound because you have always had a thirst for it.

Now, don't delay. Already it is late enough! Now, move into meditation because there, and only there, can there be a meeting with me. And not only with me – but with everything. And not only with everything – but with yourself.

112.

Love.

In love, one has to drown, because only those who drown survive.

To drown in love, in prayer, in godliness, *is* the shore. Understand it like this: if you protect yourself, you will drown; if you let yourself drown, you will survive – although how can it even be understood until you drown?

113.

Love.

Your second letter:

Mad one! In love, in prayer – it happens only in this way. The bird of the being takes off on the unknown voyage. That is the only journey worth embarking on. All else is wandering.

But wandering gives a feeling of security because it is, after all, on familiar and known paths. There is danger in the unknown. There is danger in insecurity. Ah! But life is only found in the unknown.

A grave is always beyond danger. This is why we all die before we have lived.

114.

Love.

Don't think of tomorrow. Let the future take care of the future. Just today is enough for a meditator – now is enough.

Live only in the moment. Beyond the moment only madness exists, because in reality the moment is eternity. And give each other love. Give friendliness. Give the gift of life. This is the meaning of being a husband and wife. As love grows, sex will disappear of its own accord. See the divine in each other, and then you will not see bodies. Look deeply into each other, and then you will not see what is mortal.

If partners in lovemaking cannot become partners in enlightenment, then know well that an opportunity has been wasted.

115.

Love.
Meditate about death. Meditate on death.
There is fear if you avoid death. There is fear when you escape from death. There is fearlessness when you encounter death.
Death can only be encountered in meditation. And for the one who has known death, the doors of the deathless open.

116.

Love.
It is not fear that is holding on to you. It is you who is holding on to fear.
It will drop only if you drop it. And you want the impossible: you want that fear to drop without you dropping it. This has never happened, nor can it ever. Drop it, and see.
And then you will laugh.

117.

Love.
Coincidence is a rare phenomenon in meditation. Sometimes when the traveler is there, the boat is missing. Sometimes both the boat and the traveler are there, but the river is missing. Sometimes the traveler, the boat, and the river are all there, but the boatman is missing. And, sometimes even the traveler, the boat, the

river, and the boatman are all there and yet the journey does not take place.

You are in this last state. Don't delay anymore, because it doesn't take long for such a coincidence to dissipate.

118.

Love.

Learn – learn something from every experience. Sweet or sour – all experiences make life richer.

Eventually, the experiences don't remain, only wisdom does. So keep your attention only on that which will eventually remain.

The flowers of experience will disappear; that is why one who does not extract the fragrance of wisdom from them will eventually end up empty-handed.

119.

Love.

Don't worry about the world, because aren't one's own worries enough? And don't think about others, because where has thinking about oneself ever reached an end? What will happen to religion? That is not the real question. What is happening to oneself. That, alone, is the real question.

Don't ask things that are not directly related to your own meditation, because there is no end to such things, but there is an end to you. And before you come to your ending, it is essential to know that which never ends.

120.

Love.

Certainly everything is ready. Just a spark is needed.

Once the fire has caught light it will not go out. This is not a fire that will extinguish, because it is not a material fire, it is the fire of godliness.

Burn, so that nothing is left behind, so that even the ashes cannot be found. To be burned away like that *is* nirvana.

121.

Love.

Not everything in life is understood because understanding is very small, and life is infinitely vast. What is more, if the ocean doesn't fit into the intellect's begging bowl, it isn't the ocean's fault.

Don't stop at understanding. Understanding is necessary, but not enough. The intellect certainly has a small, illuminated island – but that island is in a half-lit ocean, and that ocean is part of a totally unlit much greater ocean. The known is nothing before the unknown. And the unknown is nothing before the unknowable.

The combination of all of these is what I call godliness.

122.

Love.

Arguing comes from the intellect. Within the intellect there is no end to arguments. As long as there is thinking, there will be arguing because thinking is duality.

That is why an end to such arguments will come neither from the Vedas, the Bible, nor the Koran. There is no end to the arguments that will come from words, scriptures, and doctrines.

Non-duality is encountered beyond thought, in meditation. And that, alone, is dialogue. Dialogue does not happen before that.

So seek meditation. Seek silence. Seek enlightenment.

123.

Love.

Where there is a thirst, there is a way. With resolve, even dreams will come true, won't they?

If there is resolve, where is the gap between dream and truth?

124.

Love.

Certainly, religion is eternal – beginningless, endless – but not religious scriptures. Religious scriptures are always in time; in other words, they are temporal. Truth is beyond time, but not words. That is why religion is spoken and yet cannot be spoken.

Wittgenstein has mentioned two kinds of dialogue: saying and showing. Religious dialogue is of the second kind. Religiousness cannot be said, but only shown. Poor scriptures can merely say. Showing is not within the capacity of words. Yes, a *person* can show. That is why there are religious people, but not religious scriptures, because a person can be both within and beyond time simultaneously. But words and scriptures do not have that capacity.

Having said that, words and scriptures are not futile; because through them comes the realization of the futility of words. That is why becoming free from them is the beginning of the wordless journey.

125.

Love.

There is no other way than to leave yourself in the hands of existence.

Man is helpless about the ultimate problems of life. Try to understand this helplessness properly and accept it. That, alone, is surrender, and surrender is the solution. As long as you fight, you will be defeated. So be defeated. Be defeated by yourself. Do not wait to be defeated by death. Being defeated by oneself is the gateway to victory.

126.

Love.

If one has to hit, shouldn't one hit hard? Small hits won't do. Man's sleep is deep. Perhaps, it is less a sleep and more an unconsciousness. And, what is more, man is skilled at understanding the opposite meaning, even with hits!

Meanings that do not break your sleep will deepen it further. Poison can be used as medicine. But then medicine can also be used as poison, can't it?

127.

Love.

There is no path other than meditation. Or rather, whatever paths are there are all different forms of meditation. Prayer is also meditation, worship too, veneration too. Yoga is also meditation, and the enumerating philosophical system of Sankhya, and gyan, knowledge. Bhakti, devotion, and karma, action, are also meditation, sannyas too.

Meditation means a silent, thought-less, pure state of mind. How you attain this state is not significant. Just attaining it is significant.

By which path you become healthy is secondary. Just becoming healthy is what is important.

128.

Love.

The journey is long because the destination is near.

We see that which is far away in the distance, but our eyes never see that which is close to us. We feel a call that is coming from far away: it seems to be beckoning, it becomes a challenge to the ego. But that which is close by is simply forgotten.

That is how the being has been forgotten. That is how godliness has been forgotten. That is why the journey to what is closest to us has become the longest.

Understand this – then you won't have to walk at all.

Recognize this – then you will discover that you are already standing at the destination.

129.

Love.

Yes! I have certainly returned. I called you from the peaks, but perhaps my voice didn't reach you, or if it did, you couldn't understand it. So there was only one way: for me to return to your valleys and speak your own language. But will you be able to understand this either? Or even if you do understand it, will you understand it wrongly? You did the same with Krishna, you did the same with Buddha and so I know that nothing different will happen with me.

But if you aren't getting tired, why should I? I shall go on calling. If you don't come to my peaks, you don't. But I can certainly come to your valleys in the hope of giving you news of the luminous peaks, and of destroying your blindness, born out of the valleys' darkness.

I know very well that you will fight me, because even diseases that you have lived with for so long become your friends. How can you believe in a light that you do not know?

And you do not know me either, so how can you trust me?

130.

Love.

I am very happy with your progress.

Your sexual energy has been freed for upward movement. That was the problem but now it has resolved. From now on, the dimension of meditation will be different. Up until now even meditation was a struggle, but now it will become a let-go.

Now, you do not need to swim, Now, you are to flow. Flow – blissfully, peacefully, relaxedly, as if you do not have to reach anywhere; as if wherever you reach is the only destination.

Now, even if you drown, that will be the shore.

131.

Love.

When you leave something to existence, leave it totally. Happiness, unhappiness; leave it all to existence. Become weightless. Do not hold on to understanding either. Offer it that too and become ignorant – because

ultimately, understanding is the biggest weight!
Eventually, understanding is the biggest barrier to arise
on the path of understanding. You have given
understanding many chances, over many lifetimes – and
what have you gained? The doors to life's mysteries are
closed to understanding, but are always open for the
ignorant.
Where there is a wall for logic, there is a door for love.
Where there is defeat for the intellect, there is victory for
the heart.

132.
Love.
Religiousness is needed, not religions, because
religiousness is religious, but religions become political.
Religiousness is like love – personal, individual; not an
organization, but a search. If you want to experience it,
seek within yourself; if you want to lose it, pay attention
to others.
If you want to experience it, dig within yourself; with
meditation, with prayerfulness, with worship. Its source
is close by, very close by.
But how can those who do not even bring their
awareness close to themselves be close to godliness?

133.
Love.
Of course, there is a relationship.
Not just now, but a very ancient one, from lifetimes. This
is why you could hear the call. This is why you could
understand the language. This is why you could trust.
And slowly, slowly everything will resurface in your

memory. It has already begun. Memory doesn't die, it is only forgotten. Lifetimes of layers of memory rest in the unconscious. They will arise and engulf you. Don't be afraid of them. Don't worry about them.

Their reawakening is wholesome, benedictory.

134.

Love.

How can you meet the divine without going mad?
Going mad is the only precondition for a meeting.
Consider yourself blessed that it has called you. It will make you mad, it will demolish you. Just as the ocean calls the river, so it has invited you. Just as the river goes dancing and singing to meet its beloved, so you will have to go. Just as the river runs fearlessly in the unknown and the unacquainted, so you will have to run.

In the end, just as the river disappears into the ocean by dropping its attachment to the banks, so you will also have to disappear.

135.

Love.

In your heart, there is suppressed pain, suppressed tears.
In meditation, the pain will burst and tears will flow.
This is how you will be relieved of that weight which has frozen your being like a rock.

So do not be miserly when crying. Do not hesitate. Do not contemplate.

Weep – weep to your heart's content. Weep with your whole being. Let the pain melt and flow.

Having bathed in tears, you will become well. You are sick only because you stopped them.

136.

Love.

If the Ganges is close by, it is no longer the Ganges. Distance gives perspective. Our eyes remain closed to what is near. That is why godliness is not seen; not because it is too far away, nor because it is invisible, but only because it is nearer than the nearest. And man, thinking his blindness is its invisibility, remains content! Soon I too will go far away – I will have to go because my time is also borrowed. Then you will be able to see me rightly because distance gives perspective.

Soon the boat to carry me to the other shore will dock at this shore, and the call of *the one* who has sent me will come. Then you will be able to recognize me properly. At the moment of my departure, your mind will have no doubts, and trust will arise toward one who is disappearing into the beyond.

Doubts are mind's safety measures. Mistrust is its protection. Perhaps what you are unable to receive when you are near me, you will be able to receive when I am far away. But I want you to take it while I am near. Otherwise, your heart will repent greatly and you will unnecessarily drown in many tears.

137.

Love.

No, I will not be leaving soon. I will leave only after completing the work I have come for, or have been sent for. But just because I will not be leaving soon doesn't mean that you don't need to hurry up.

If you delay, then even my later than late will prove to be soon. And if you hurry, then even my soon will be late.

Think! No – what will come of thinking? Do something in search of yourself. Walk a little toward yourself.

138.

Love.

The paths toward attaining truth are infinite, and which one is suitable for each individual depends on him. That is why what is right for one person may be completely wrong for another. That is why calm, gentle patience is needed with the other. It is dangerous to think of oneself as the criterion for all.

I see the expression of this very truth in *anekantvad,* the philosophy of multiplicity, or in *syatvad,* the philosophy of perhapsism. The path of a thinking-oriented person is not the same as the path of a feeling-oriented person. What is a door to the extrovert is a wall to the introvert.

The pilgrim of knowledge eventually makes meditation his boat. The pilgrim of love makes prayerfulness his boat. Meditation and prayer arrive at the same destination, but their routes are utterly different.

It is only right that you choose your route and are not bothered about others, because when it is so difficult even to understand oneself, then to understand the other will be almost impossible.

139.

Love.

Aloneness is a fact of life. One can awaken from it, but one cannot avoid it. It is always with us, like a shadow. A shadow, at least, gives company in the dark, but aloneness manifests even more intensely in the dark. In the dark, perhaps man is more afraid of his aloneness and less of the darkness.

So don't run from or avoid aloneness. Rather, live it. It is. Embrace it. If you deny that which is, nothing but misery will follow.

Accepting that which is, is the only bliss. And that alone is religiousness.

140.

Love.

The evening had descended. The sun had set. The master said to the disciple, "Go inside and put the scripture in the cupboard."

The disciple went. But he returned at once, terrified, and said to the master, "Beloved master, there is a snake in the cupboard!"

The master replied, "Here is a mantra to drive the snake away – go and chant it, and the snake will disappear."

The disciple went. He chanted the mantra. But he returned even more terrified, saying, "Beloved master, the snake is more powerful than the mantra. I chanted the mantra, but the snake is still lying where it was."

The master replied, "You may not have chanted it with trust."

The disciple went again. He chanted the mantra again. But he returned running, more terrified than ever, and said, "Beloved master, I even chanted it with trust, but the snake still doesn't move!"

The master replied, "Then drop the mantra and take a lamp."

The disciple returned from the cupboard laughing with a rope in his hand.

Don't fight sexual desire. Don't fight any desire. The mantra of fighting will not work. The lamp: simply take in the lamp of meditation – nothing but that will help. Desire is life-energy seen in darkness. Desire is looking in darkness, in ignorance. In the light of meditation, the snake of desire is simply not found. In the light of meditation you find that which is. In the darkness of ignorance – or in the blindness of the absence of meditation – you see that which certainly is not.

Light the lamp of meditation and go in. And I will wait for the moment when you come out laughing, saying, "The snake is just not there."

141.

Love.

Through ignorance, even blessings become curses, and through understanding, even curses become blessings. That is why the real question is not of curses or blessings; the real question is knowing the alchemy which transforms thorns into flowers. Coal that passes through a chemical process becomes a diamond. Sannyas is such a process that turns coal-like consciousness into diamonds. I am revealing the fundamental key of the alchemy of sannyas to you. I will not say it directly. I will certainly say it – and yet you will also have to *look* for it, because an indirect indication is an essential part of revealing that key. Some great mantras are such that they just cannot be said directly. Or if they are said, they cannot be understood. Or if they are understood, their intrinsic poetry is lost. That poetry is their very soul.

Every morning before dawn, Eknath used to go for a

bath in the Godavari River. As soon as he got out from his bath, someone would spit on him. Eknath would laugh and take another bath.

The self-appointed masters of religion had hired a man to do this. But, there was one condition: he would only get his reward if Eknath could be made angry.

One day, two days, a week, two weeks… All that man's efforts were being made in vain. Finally, he made a last attempt. One day he spat on Eknath one hundred and seven times. Eknath laughed each time and took another bath.

Then the man spat for the one hundred and eighth time. Eknath laughed and took a fresh bath. Then he returned and stood in front of the man – in anticipation, perhaps, that he would spit again, but the poor man was really tired. His mouth had gone dry from spitting again and again.

Eknath waited for a while with a prayerful heart, and then he said, "How can I find the words to thank you? Earlier, I used to enjoy the bliss of Godavari's lap only once, but because of your virtuous inspiration I began to have it twice. And what to say of today? I have had the blessing of bathing one hundred and eight times in the Godavari. The work is yours but I am reaping the fruits!"

142.

Love.

Trusting in energy is more powerful than the energy itself. Energy on its own has no life. Trusting in oneself gives life to it. Energy on its own is just a body – the soul comes from valuing oneself.

Not only is energy devoid of trust lifeless; energy devoid of trust is also suicidal. This is because energy that is not creative engages in destruction, and first of all in self-destruction. This is because unused energy takes revenge upon itself, and, mistrust in the self doesn't allow energy to flow in useful creative dimensions.

When I see you, I am always reminded of an incident from the Mahabharata:

The battle between Karna and Arjuna was hugely unequal because it was a battle between the sun and Indra. What is poor Indra in relation to the sun? But that which was expected to happen did not happen, and what did not seem likely to happen did happen.

Karna was badly defeated, and this happened because he made Shalya his charioteer. *Shalya* means doubt, apprehension, *karna* means ear. After all, every doubt enters through the path of your ears; your ears are the doors to doubt.

Shalya kept saying to Karna, "How will you defeat Arjuna?" So Karna was defeated and doubt won.

Avoid Shalya. There is absolutely no need to make him your charioteer.

143.

Love.

A long time ago, there was an amazing businessman in Arabia. He had never known failure. Whatever he touched would turn into gold. People thought he was some kind of a magician, and he was, because whenever he ventured on a journey, leaving his pleasure palace behind for a time, his camels would return weighed down with loads of new treasures.

Sometimes they would return loaded with diamonds and pearls, sometimes with gold and gold coins, and sometimes with the most beautiful damsels.

Then one day, the rumor went around that this amazing businessman had revealed the secret of his success in a book. Naturally, a crowd of thousands thronged at his door. The businessman not only acknowledged that he had revealed the secret of his success in a book, but he also said that he himself had read this magical book regularly over the past fifty years.

Finally he said, "If you follow my advice, your lives too will become as miraculous as mine." But when he opened the book to show it to the crowd, who were almost mad in their eagerness to see it, only seven words were repeatedly written in that big book.

I want to say those seven words to you. They are: "Whatever happens, always try just one more time."

144.

Love.

Now, you may be anywhere, but you will still be here. Space will make no difference, time will no longer be a wall. Physical distance will not create a distance, nor will physical nearness create nearness.

You are entering a completely different dimension – the dimensionless dimension – where there is no multiplicity, no duality. Only "I" is there; not the "I" that is visible from the outside, nor the "I" that is the boundary line of "thou," but rather the "I" which is also "thou."

"*Tattvamasi*, Shvetaketu" – "That art thou, Shvetaketu."

145.

Love.

Gather courage.

Courage is not something that is already there, rather, it is born from being courageous. Fear is also not already there. It is the complexity that results from not gathering courage.

You have already experienced not gathering courage – the fear, like a fog over your being, is proof enough of that. Now, experience gathering courage. On the one hand, the sun of courage is rising and on the other, the fog of fear is disappearing.

And, remember that only fearlessness is soul.

146.

Love.

You ask how to make the invisible visible?

Pay attention to the visible. Don't just look, pay attention. This means that when you see a flower, let your whole being become the eye. When you listen to the birds, let your entire body–soul become the ear. When you look at a flower, do not think. When you listen to birds, do not ponder.

Let your total consciousness either see or hear or smell or taste or touch. Because it is due to a shallow sensitivity that the invisible does not become visible, and the unknown remains unknown.

Deepen your sensitivity. Don't just swim in sensitivity, drown in it. This, I call meditation. And in meditation, the seen disappears and, finally, the seer too. Then only seeing remains.

In this seeing the invisible becomes visible and the

unknown, known. Not only this, even the unknowable becomes knowable. Remember not to start thinking about whatever I am writing – act.

Nothing has ever been, nor can ever be, attained by theoreticians. There is no other door except seeing for oneself.

147.

Love.

There was an amazing master, Shoichi. From the day he began teaching in the Tofuku temple, it was transformed. The day would come and the day would go, the night would come and the night would go, but the temple would remain still and silent.

That temple became a deep silence. Not the faintest sound arose from it. No longer were sutras chanted from the scriptures, no longer was there worship and prayer. Even the temple bells stood still – no one touched them, because the disciples of Shoichi did not do anything except meditation.

It remained like this for years. People even forgot that there was a temple nearby. Hundreds of sannyasins were there; and much was happening, yet, all was silence and emptiness.

Great things would happen there: lamps of self-realization would alight, flowers of enlightenment would bloom. Yet, all was silence and emptiness.

Then one day, people heard the temple bells ringing and sutras from the scriptures being chanted. What was this unbelievable happening? They ran toward the temple. The whole town gathered at its door.

Shoichi had left this world. Sutras from the scriptures

were being chanted, and bells were being rung over his dead body.

People were astonished, but I think it was only right, because as long as a temple is alive, it is silent.

148.

Love.

Meditation is inaction as well as action; an inaction that is not opposed to action, and an action whose center is inaction. When there is no sense of the doer within, this miraculous state happens all by itself. The presence of the witness is the absence of the doer.

There was a master, Hotei. He was one of a kind – but when are masters ever of anyone else's kind? He had no ashram, no temple, no monastery, no disciples. The roads were his home, his ashram, his temple, and his monastery. A bag on his shoulder, he would wander the roads all day long. There were fruits, sweets, and toys in his bag. He would distribute them to the children and dance, sing, and laugh with them. He would tell them stories that would sow seeds of meditation in them. In his presence, children would drop into meditation. Wherever he stopped on the road became a sacred place. Travelers would pass by silently and reverently. Hotei was living meditation; wherever he stood was a temple. To the passing travelers who love meditation he would say, "A penny for meditation, please!" and his bag would soon fill with coins. Sometimes, someone would ask him to come to a temple and preach religion to the people, to which he would laugh and say, "One penny more, please, for the temple."

His name would reach every house, no matter which village he was passing through. Children became his messengers: their faces aflame with a light from the beyond and flowers of unique bliss blooming in their eyes. Whenever Hotei passed through a place so did a laughing meditation. Slowly, slowly people forgot his name and started knowing him as "The Laughing Buddha."

One day, in some village, a religious scholar stopped him on his way and asked him, "What is meditation?"

He must have been certain that Hotei would quote the scriptures and give a definition of meditation, but instead Hotei gave a belly laugh, dropped his bag onto the ground, closed his eyes, and disappeared into meditation. Tears of bliss started flowing from his eyes. Only his body remained in that place – he himself was transported to some other land.

Ah! What he gave was the right answer, but the scholar did not understand it. By all accounts, it is difficult to find a more ignorant person than a scholar! So the scholar shook Hotei, disturbed his meditation, and asked again, "Practically speaking, what is meditation?" as if the answer that Hotei had given was impractical.

Hotei laughed again, put his bag on his shoulder, bowed down in greeting to the scholar, and proceeded on his journey.

The sound of his departing footsteps had the same peace as his silence. This was his answer to the second question!

149.

Love.

Auspicious are the symptoms and invaluable the opportunity.

Surrender to existence and carry on. This light will keep growing until eventually there will be only an immense light, and the darkness will have simply disappeared. There is no darkness except our ignorance. And where there is no ignorance – no darkness – there is no ego either; simply the ocean, not the drop.

A music without instruments will shower on you just as a fragrance without flowers is showering now.

The soundless sound is close by. Keep going. Keep moving ahead with a prayerful heart.

Auspicious are the symptoms and invaluable the opportunity.

150.

Love.

The bliss of meditation is unique, the experience of bliss otherworldly – as if those doors that seem to have been forever closed have reopened, and a friendly sun is shining into what was once an unfathomable darkness. The heart's bud suddenly becomes a flower and soundless music plays on the being's inner strings. Each and every breath is dancing, every fiber of one's bodymind is singing.

Be grateful. Be filled with delight. Thank existence. Let your whole being say: "The grace of existence is infinite."

About Osho

Osho's unique contribution to the understanding of who we are defies categorization. Mystic and scientist, a rebellious spirit whose sole interest is to alert humanity to the urgent need to discover a new way of living. To continue as before is to invite threats to our very survival on this unique and beautiful planet.

His essential point is that only by changing ourselves, one individual at a time, can the outcome of all our "selves" – our societies, our cultures, our beliefs, our world – also change. The doorway to that change is meditation.

Osho the scientist has experimented and scrutinized all

the approaches of the past and examined their effects on the modern human being and responded to their shortcomings by creating a new starting point for the hyperactive 21st Century mind: OSHO Active Meditations.

Once the agitation of a modern lifetime has started to settle, "activity" can melt into "passivity," a key starting point of real meditation. To support this next step, Osho has transformed the ancient "art of listening" into a subtle contemporary methodology: the OSHO Talks. Here words become music, the listener discovers who is listening, and the awareness moves from what is being heard to the individual doing the listening. Magically, as silence arises, what needs to be heard is understood directly, free from the distraction of a mind that can only interrupt and interfere with this delicate process.

These thousands of talks cover everything from the individual quest for meaning to the most urgent social and political issues facing society today. Osho's books are not written but are transcribed from audio and video recordings of these extemporaneous talks to international audiences. As he puts it, "So remember: whatever I am saying is not just for you...I am talking also for the future generations."

Osho has been described by *The Sunday Times* in London as one of the "1000 Makers of the 20th Century" and by American author Tom Robbins as "the most dangerous man since Jesus Christ." *Sunday Mid-Day* (India) has selected Osho as one of ten people – along with Gandhi, Nehru and Buddha – who have changed the destiny of India.

About his own work Osho has said that he is helping to create the conditions for the birth of a new kind of human being. He often characterizes this new human being as "Zorba the Buddha" – capable both of enjoying the earthy pleasures of a Zorba the Greek and the silent serenity of a Gautama the Buddha.

Running like a thread through all aspects of Osho's talks and meditations is a vision that encompasses both the timeless wisdom of all ages past and the highest potential of today's (and tomorrow's) science and technology.

Osho is known for his revolutionary contribution to the science of inner transformation, with an approach to meditation that acknowledges the accelerated pace of contemporary life. His unique OSHO Active Meditations™ are designed to first release the accumulated stresses of body and mind, so that it is then easier to take an experience of stillness and thought-free relaxation into daily life.

Two autobiographical works by the author are available:
Autobiography of a Spiritually Incorrect Mystic,
St Martins Press, New York (book and eBook)
Glimpses of a Golden Childhood,
OSHO Media International, Pune, India (book and eBook)

OSHO International Meditation Resort

Each year the Meditation Resort welcomes thousands of people from more than 100 countries. The unique campus provides an opportunity for a direct personal experience of a new way of living – with more awareness, relaxation, celebration and creativity. A great variety of around-the-clock and around-the-year program options are available. Doing nothing and just relaxing is one of them!

All of the programs are based on Osho's vision of "Zorba the Buddha" – a qualitatively new kind of human being who is able *both* to participate creatively in everyday life *and* to relax into silence and meditation.

Location

Located 100 miles southeast of Mumbai in the thriving modern city of Pune, India, the OSHO International Meditation Resort is a holiday destination with a difference. The Meditation Resort is spread over 28 acres of spectacular gardens in a beautiful tree-lined residential area.

OSHO Meditations

A full daily schedule of meditations for every type of person includes both traditional and revolutionary methods, and particularly the OSHO Active Meditations™. The daily meditation program takes place in what must be the world's largest meditation hall, the OSHO Auditorium.

OSHO Multiversity

Individual sessions, courses and workshops cover everything from creative arts to holistic health, personal transformation, relationship and life transition, transforming meditation into a lifestyle for life and work, esoteric sciences, and the "Zen" approach to sports and recreation. The secret of the OSHO Multiversity's success lies in the fact that all its programs are combined with meditation, supporting the understanding that as human beings we are far more than the sum of our parts.

OSHO Basho Spa

The luxurious Basho Spa provides for leisurely open-air swimming surrounded by trees and tropical green. The uniquely styled, spacious Jacuzzi, the saunas, gym, tennis courts...all these are enhanced by their stunningly beautiful setting.

Cuisine

A variety of different eating areas serve delicious Western, Asian and Indian vegetarian food – most of it organically grown especially for the Meditation Resort. Breads and cakes are baked in the resort's own bakery.

Night life

There are many evening events to choose from – dancing being at the top of the list! Other activities include full-moon meditations beneath the stars, variety shows, music performances and meditations for daily life.

Facilities

You can buy all of your basic necessities and toiletries in

the Galleria. The Multimedia Gallery sells a large range of OSHO media products. There is also a bank, a travel agency and a Cyber Café on-campus. For those who enjoy shopping, Pune provides all the options, ranging from traditional and ethnic Indian products to all of the global brand-name stores.

Accommodation

You can choose to stay in the elegant rooms of the OSHO Guesthouse, or for longer stays on campus you can select one of the OSHO Living-In programs. Additionally there is a plentiful variety of nearby hotels and serviced apartments.

www.osho.com/meditationresort
www.osho.com/guesthouse
www.osho.com/livingin

For More Information

www.**OSHO**.com

a comprehensive multi-language website including a magazine, OSHO Books, OSHO Talks in audio and video formats, the OSHO Library text archive in English and Hindi and extensive information about OSHO Meditations. You will also find the program schedule of the OSHO Multiversity and information about the OSHO International Meditation Resort.

http://OSHO.com/AllAboutOSHO
http://OSHO.com/Resort
http://OSHO.com/Shop
http://www.youtube.com/OSHO
http://www.Twitter.com/OSHO
http://www.facebook.com/pages/OSHO.International

To contact OSHO International Foundation:
www.osho.com/oshointernational,
oshointernational@oshointernational.com